IN YOUR STARS

Discover the essence of astrology

igloobooks

igloobooks

Designed by Simon Parker
Edited by Natalie Graham

Copyright © 2020 Igloo Books Ltd

Published in 2020
First published in the UK by Igloo Books Ltd
An imprint of Igloo Books Ltd
Cottage Farm, NN6 0BJ, UK
Owned by Bonnier Books
Sveavägen 56, Stockholm, Sweden

Manufactured in China. 1020 001
10 9 8 7 6 5 4 3 2 1

Library of Congress Cataloging-in-Publication
Data is available upon request.

ISBN 978-1-83903-783-2
IglooBooks.com
bonnierbooks.co.uk

CONTENTS

THE SUN SIGNS

No matter when your birthday is, you were born under a Sun sign, and you almost certainly know which of the twelve signs of the Zodiac you belong to. In the simplest terms, that's what the ancient discipline of astrology is. Since our earliest ancestors, humankind has looked up to the heavens and wondered what kind of influence they have on our lives. While astrology – as the study of the skies is known – is thousands of years old, it is definitely experiencing a wave of popularity today.

A BRIEF HISTORY

More than 4,000 years ago, Babylonian priests in the ancient Mesopotamian city-state would predict the future using different methods, such as studying the entrails of slaughtered animals and charting the movement of the stars and planets in the dark night sky. With the invention of mathematics in Mesopotamia around 3000 BCE, priests began to plot detailed tables to chart these heavenly movements. Written in Babylonian cuneiform, these were the earliest known birth charts made by man. Centuries of refinement followed until, by the eighth century BCE, the libraries in Babylon held more than 7,000 astrological warnings. The Babylonians' sophisticated understanding of mathematics meant that they were the astrological leaders of the ancient world and by 500 BCE, had invented the Zodiac we still use today.

Over the next several hundred years, first the ancient Egyptians and then the ancient Greeks refined astrology until, by the second century BCE, it contained the elements that make up astrology as we understand it today: a horoscope or birth chart that contained the position of the stars at the precise moment of birth. The Sun, the Moon and the then-known planets were set against the circle of the Zodiac, and the concept of one sign being in ascendance – rising over the horizon – at the moment of birth was born.

A ROYAL BIRTH

The horoscope you have read in your daily newspaper or online is actually a fairly recent and a very simplified invention that owes its existence to a royal baby. In 1930, a Sunday newspaper commissioned the astrologer R.H. Naylor to write the horoscope of the newly born Princess Margaret. His horoscope proved so popular he was asked to write more. When he correctly predicted an air disaster later that year, Naylor was rewarded with a weekly

horoscope slot. In order to make his interpretations easily understandable, Naylor invented the star-sign column of astrology we still use today. He placed each sign in the position of the first astrological house starting with Aries, the first sign of the Zodiac. In order to fit the format of newspapers and magazines, Naylor's version of astrology was a huge over-simplification.

Over the course of this book, we will show how much we can learn about ourselves from reading not just our star signs, but by also plotting our birth charts. Let's start at the beginning.

THE TWELVE SIGNS

Astrology is based on the idea that the movement of the stars and other celestial bodies, such as the planets, have an effect on our lives. While many people are sceptical about the power of astrology to affect our daily lives, they cannot deny scientific facts such as the Moon's influence on Earth's ocean tides, which shows how the celestial and terrestrial connect. Perhaps part of the reason for scepticism is that people misunderstand astrology as determining our fate and see it as removing our free will. In fact, astrology describes our potential. By learning to read and understand the complex symbols contained within our individual and unique birth charts, we can unlock the potential in our lives. Despite what you might think reading your daily horoscope, astrology's job isn't to tell us what will happen on a daily basis. It is meant to show us trends and patterns that govern our lives and help us to gain a deeper insight and knowledge of ourselves, so that we can be our truest selves.

The astrological signs and symbols are a little more than astrological shorthand. Once you know your sign, you know what to look for – and it makes understanding your horoscope, on astrology's simplest level, easy! Once you can recognize the symbols for the planets and aspects, it allows you to read your much more detailed and complex birth charts.

THE HOROSCOPE

The Zodiac is divided into twelve houses. Why? Our ancestors looked at the sky and saw the Sun, Moon, and planets and thought they revolved around the Earth. We now know better, and while the ancients were wrong, if you look at the Sun, it does look as though it revolves around the Earth; rising in the east and setting in the west; never veering from the ribbon of space that encircles the Earth like a huge hoop. In fact, this strip of space known as the ecliptic provides the form for the Zodiac. Think of it as a huge circle or a large pie that divides into 360 degrees, with each degree split into 60 minutes. The Zodiac is divided into twelve equal parts, meaning each part is thirty degrees. Each thirty-degree part of the circle is called a 'house,' and over a year, just like with our calendar, the Sun will travel through the twelve houses, passing from one house to the next until it has traveled through all twelve. The houses are not synchronized with our calendar months, and to make matters more complicated, the cusp – the division between one house and the next – can vary by a day or two from one horoscope to the next.

The twelve houses of the Zodiac are what we call our star or Sun signs. It means that your sign is the one that the Sun occupied when you were born. So, if you were born on March 30, you would belong to Aries, the first sign of the Zodiac. Ancient astrologers divided the twelve signs of the Zodiac into groups of three, each represented by one of four elements: fire, earth, air, and water – the four basic elements of life. Without these four elements, we would not exist.

Fire signs are Aries the Ram, Leo the Lion, and Sagittarius the Archer, and they are connected by the life force that fire brings. The earth signs are pragmatic and productive and include Taurus the Bull, Virgo the Virgin, and Capricorn the Goat. Gemini the Twins, Libra the Scales, and Aquarius the Water Bearer make up

the air signs, the intellectual heart of the Zodiac. Last but not least
are the water signs, the most mutable and sensitive of all the star
signs, Cancer the Crab, Scorpio the Scorpion, and Pisces the Fish,
the twelfth sign of the horoscope.

ARIES THE RAM

MARCH 21–APRIL 20

SNAPSHOT

Element: Fire

Quality: Cardinal

Keywords: Leader, pioneer

Planetary Ruler: Mars

Rules: Head, face

The first of the twelve signs of the Zodiac, Aries the Ram shares its first day with the first day of the astrological year and the spring equinox. The sign of new beginnings, Aries is not to be messed with. Like a ram, it can lock its horns, and also act like a battering ram until it gets its way and the job is done.

CHARACTER

Aries' many strengths are also its weaknesses. Ruled by the head, a typical Aries is as stubborn as its sign, the Ram. Full of energy and a zest for life, an Aries is always passionate and enthusiastic about everything. They are natural-born leaders and approach all that life throws at them with not just courage, but also with a sense of purpose. They make snap

decisions and never look back with regret, even if the decision is later proved to be wrong. Their philosophy is that life is too short to wallow in indecision and regret. Their rule in every aspect of their life is to not overthink any situation. Instead, they grasp it quickly and deal with it accordingly. While other signs might applaud their boldness, others might see Aries as too aggressive and pushy.

Always bold, resourceful, and courageous, a typical Aries is a born survivor. Their will to succeed and their ambition will often drive them to a positive end result, but their lack of persistence means they may give up on a project if it takes too long to get the result they want. However, their enthusiasm means that others are happy to go along with them and help them achieve the desired result.

Aries wants action; they always want to take the lead and have others follow them as they break new ground. Challenges are there to be met and not shied away from. The planets in Aries encourage them to act spontaneously and take whatever risks are necessary to succeed.

THE DOWNSIDE

Losing is something Aries hates just about as much as compromising. It's their way or no way. When things don't go according to plan, Aries can be surprisingly naïve and unable to understand others' positions. This can lead to others seeing Aries as a little inconsiderate. Their legendary impatience, coupled with a lack of thoroughness and foresight, leads to accusations of self-absorption and self-centeredness. Long-term planning is not an Arian skill and, when added to their inability to listen to others, Aries can be frustrating company. But, take them on their terms and they can save any kind of situation by remaining cool and collected in an emergency, because they make decisions speedily and without the need to consult others. That's how confident Aries are in their ability and their vision.

LOVE

In love as in life, Aries pursues the object of their affections with great determination. Not for nothing is Aries the first sign of the twelve: they are the playboys and playgirls of the Zodiac. Where they lead others will follow. Once they have decided on their partner, they will try their hardest to win their love. Then, once they are established in a relationship, they will show great warmth and love to their chosen ones. Their almost impossibly high levels of self-belief can be very attractive to other signs. But just as they are passionate in every part of their lives, they can lose interest when their passion dims as fast as it rose. A relationship with an Aries will never be boring!

An Aries will typically take charge in the relationship – they love being the top dog. They fall in love easily and often make mistakes (which they would never admit to) along the way before they find the 'right' one. Once they have the 'one,' they will do everything in their power to make them feel as special as they possibly can.

The downside to a relationship with an Aries is that they can easily become jealous. Their desire to be all things to their lover can leave some partners feeling a little overwhelmed.

ARIES WOMAN

An Aries woman is driven in love just as in life. She will use all her feminine wiles to get the object of her affections. Her ability to seduce is legendary. She pursues the goals she sets in both her personal and professional life with boundless energy, although once her initial enthusiasm fades away, she may not hang around unless she can keep up her interest levels. In any relationship, including love matches, an Aries woman will always want equality. Men hold no fear for an Aries woman who sees herself as an equal in all things. As a result, men are attracted to her because of her air of confidence.

ARIES MAN

Just like an Aries woman, an Aries man is supremely confident and projects an image of success even when he's notched up failures. He loves extremes of anything and challenges himself on every level, driven by his own self-belief and impatience to get as much out of life as possible. He has complete confidence in his own judgement and abilities when making decisions, including in his love life. He will go to any lengths to woo the partner of his choice. Perhaps surprisingly, an Aries man can be very sensitive to his lover. He is always generous, and his partner will lack for nothing.

FAMILY AND FRIENDS

Aries are known for their loyalty. As a family member and as a friend, they will always be loyal and trustworthy, and they make a great friend for that very reason, even if sometimes their unswervingly honest approach to life can be a bit too much for other people.

You will never be bored if you have an Aries friend. They are the ones who come up with madcap plans and expect you to follow. They love extreme sports and challenging themselves physically and mentally, and want their friends to do the same. An Aries will be the first to sign up for a marathon when they haven't run for years and will persuade you to join them. The only problem is that if the training doesn't go according to plan, they will give up and leave you to carry on alone. But their competitive nature means that they will most likely run the race – even if they haven't done the training!

If you become friends with an Aries, then it will be a friendship for life. Aries are generous with their time and willingly help their friends to achieve goals they might have thought impossible. Being friends with an Aries is also flattering; Aries like to surround themselves with interesting people.

Aries are most likely to befriend Geminis, Leos, Sagittarians, and Aquarians. However, they have a tricky relationship with both Cancer and Capricorn. Capricorn is too inflexible and regimented for the spontaneity-loving Aries. Cancer can be a bit too sensitive and moody for the insensitive and feisty Aries.

As parents, Aries are exciting and brave. They love to lead their families into new adventures. Sometimes, they can be a little insensitive and bossy to their children because they want their children to embrace life just like them. An Aries sibling can be annoying to their brothers and sisters; no matter what position they are in the family pecking order, their need to be the boss and take charge can be irritating. Aries are known for their short temper, but they are also known for the quickness with which they forget the reason they lost their temper in the first place!

Boundless enthusiasm and generosity are a hallmark of Aries. They will happily pay for events and take great pleasure in seeing those around them enjoy themselves. They like nothing more than gathering the people closest to them together to celebrate life. Their love of being the center of attention sits well with this. Aries love the sound of their own voice, particularly at parties and dinners, and they tell it as it is. Their inability to listen is legendary but their charm lets them get away with being an indifferent audience.

ARIES MOTHER

An Aries mother will do everything that she can to let her children know that she loves them. A fantastic communicator, she is a very affectionate woman, and this makes motherhood very easy for her. She loves to spoil her children and hug them all the time. A child with an Aries mother will always feel loved.

ARIES FATHER

An Aries father wants his children to grow up like him, because he feels he has life worked out. He will try to make his children as similar to himself as he can because he is proud of the traits that he has, not because of vanity. He would like his children to be ambitious and energetic, busy yet kind.

HEALTH AND WELLBEING

Aries exudes positivity, and this reflects well on their general health and wellbeing. They see the glass as half-full and their positive attitude extends to every aspect of their life. They like to test their strength and stamina, which means that they take good care of their health and try to stay well. When Aries get ill, they tend to get better more quickly than other signs.

Known as the sign that likes to play and work hard, Aries need to make sure they take time to rest and recover, especially after an intense workout. They also need to make sure they eat a balanced diet. Eating on the run is not to be recommended for Aries; enjoying food and eating it slowly is key. Aries don't really need stimulants such as coffee and alcohol to enjoy life; they find life stimulating enough. Having said that, as a fire sign, Aries like nothing more than hot and spicy foods. Once in a while this is great, but too often and Aries' already-stimulated system will go into overdrive. Known for their love of indulgence, Aries find that they can easily gain weight, so they need to remember to keep an eye on the waistline!

Aries rules the head and face. These are the weakest parts of the body for an Aries. Tension headaches, dizziness, earache, and skin complaints are common ailments. Many migraine and allergy sufferers are born under Aries. They need to slow down and take a deep breath to avoid getting sick!

MONEY AND CAREERS

Aries are born leaders and will excel in any career that needs a leadership role. Natural self-starters and very effective leaders, they willingly delegate responsibility and give orders, but they aren't really interested in power for its own sake. They are constantly coming up with ideas and they like nothing more than a new challenge or responsibility. Innovation and experimentation are second nature to an Aries. However, their lack of staying power can mean that once a project is underway and progressing, Aries will lose interest. They want to move on to the next big thing and leave others to see the project through to its conclusion.

As self-starters, Aries like to be their own boss and set their own schedule. They like careers where their reputation is put on the line and where they are able to challenge themselves on a daily basis. Medicine, particularly surgery, is one career that suits Aries, and anything that involves fire is a must for the fire sign.

Surprisingly perhaps, money is not a key motivator for Aries when they choose a career. Aries are not very good with money. If they have it, they spend it. Learning to save money does not come naturally to them. They see money as a means to help them enjoy life to the fullest. Because of their willingness to take risks and their entrepreneurial streak, Aries can make a lot of money, but whether they hang onto it is another question.

TAURUS THE BULL

APRIL 21–MAY 20

SNAPSHOT:

Element: Earth

Quality: Fixed

Keywords: Stubborn, endurance, perseverance

Planetary Ruler: Venus

Rules: Neck and throat

The second sign of the Zodiac, Taurus the Bull, is the first earth sign and its grounded quality provides a complementary contrast to fiery Aries' trailblazing ways. The most stubborn of all the signs, Taurus is calm and measured in every aspect of life.

CHARACTER

Taurus is the first earth sign, and this tells us everything we need to know about the Bull. Taureans are invariably cautious and reliable, and will always take a conservative approach to everything they do. Unlike Aries, Taurus is infinitely patient and pursues any goal with a single-minded determination. They will see through a task until the very end, or until they get what they want. In any race, Taurus will still be running when many other signs have long since fallen by the wayside.

17

As a result, they often achieve just what they set out to achieve. Taurus is nothing if not patient!

Ruled by the planet Venus, nice things really matter to a Taurus. They don't have to be expensive, but they often are; they appreciate the finer aspects of life, be it a soft cashmere sweater or a freshly baked sourdough loaf. With a creative streak, Taurus often displays talent in any one of the art forms and, as a result, they understand and appreciate the skill of craftspeople and artists. Naturally acquisitive, Taureans like to own nice things and will happily pay over the odds for unique objects that have been handmade. The best really matters to Taureans but, at the same time, they take great delight in simple pleasures, such as going for a walk in a beautiful forest. It helps if it's the most beautiful forest around and not just a bit of scrubland!

Taurus doesn't like to be rushed – ever. And once they make up their mind about anything, they won't change it. That's because they will have spent so long making up their mind, there's every chance they will have made the right decision. Along with their calm, measured approach to life, they want security.

THE DOWNSIDE

All the qualities that make Taurus who they are can be seen in a negative light. Their leisurely pace is just too slow for some people. Their refusal to change their mind can be seen as pig-headedness by some and it does, on occasions, mean that they fall into terrible ruts. Their love of the finer things in life makes some Taureans greedy, status-obsessed, and self-indulgent. Taurus tends to gluttony; they like their food and drink too much!

While it takes a lot to make a Taurus angry, when they do lose their temper, boy do you know about it. Their bullish behavior can be truly scary. But with Venus as their ruling sign, Taureans are more likely to be sensitive and romantic.

LOVE

Taureans are the old-fashioned lovers of the Zodiac. They like nothing more than romantic, candlelit dinners and long walks that end with them in a cozy bar, having a meal with their loved one. A Taurus will never be a player; they aren't going to be downloading multiple dating apps – they play for keeps. They combine their sensitivity with a sensible approach when looking for a romantic partner. They hate any kind of change, so they take their time finding their life partner because they have to make sure that the relationship is the one. Once they commit, they commit, and they expect the same in return. Once in a relationship, they want a stable, loyal partner who loves the sensual world as much as they do.

Taureans prize loyalty, comfort, and persistence, and that's what they will look for in love. A relationship is a bit like a project for them. They are attentive, self-sacrificing, and caring with their partner. Dependable and reliable, a Taurus loves to be needed. No sacrifice is too great, and they will always be there to help out in any way that's needed, just as long as they never feel they are being taken for granted.

A Taurus will do everything to avoid conflict if they possibly can. The endless romantic dramas that Leo and Scorpio thrive off are not for them. Sometimes, their intensity and sincerity can come across as being a little over-possessive and jealous. That's because, for a Taurean, love has never been a game – but the essence of life.

TAURUS WOMAN

Ruled by Venus, Taurus women are endlessly romantic. They love all those clichéd symbols; they want that special someone to shower them with flowers, chocolates, weekends away, moonlit walks on the beach, and candle-lit dinners. The more, the better. However, that's not enough to win a Taurus woman's heart. She is looking for a partner with the sophistication and class that she values, someone who will work hard to keep the relationship passionate and dynamic and who is in it for the long term. They are generous and thoughtful with their partner, but woe betide anyone who mistakenly thinks they can make a Taurus woman change her opinion. Don't ever back her into a corner. She won't back down and she won't forget.

TAURUS MAN

Taurean men project an image of a steady, reliable partner and that's just as well – because that is exactly what you will get. They want familiarity and the day-to-day contentment a long-term relationship brings. They don't want fireworks and the endless drama of different partners. For them, the domestic daily rituals are deeply romantic. Sharing life's better things with a long-term partner is as good as it gets for a Taurus man.

FAMILY AND FRIENDS

Being friends with a Taurus is special. It might take some time before a Taurus will accept you into their inner circle, because Taurus treat friends like family. They value friendship; they not only remember when your birthday is, they send a card. Befriending a Taurus needs staying power, and they are so set in their ways that they might turn down your invitation the first couple of times because their diary is full. But persist! Once a Taurus makes a friend, you become a friend for life. Non-judgmental and kind, they are there to scoop you up when disaster strikes. Knowing the value of a good meal, they will feed you in times of crisis and spoil you when you need your spirits restored.

Since Taurus loves routine, they are happy to meet up with their friends on a weekly basis whether it's to play sport, see a film, or have a meal, so they can keep up with your life and you can keep up with theirs. Taurus loves detail and loves to know that their friends are as interested in them as they are in you. Sometimes, this can come over as clingy and possessive. They don't mean to be jealous, but to some their sincerity

can be just a bit too much. Just remember that Taurus is sincere above everything and means well.

Loyal and dependable Taureans are happiest in a domestic setting and put both their family and friends at the center of their world. For Taurus, finding a partner is essential to smooth the pathway to a long and happy life as part of a family. Children are a key part of the Taurean life plan, whether they are their own children, nieces and nephews, godchildren, or friends' kids. Life is better for Taurus with children in it and they will always include kids in their social plans.

Coming home to a family after work is what it is all about for Taurus and makes the hours away from home worthwhile. Taurus likes to be involved in every aspect of family life and is more than happy to spend any free time doing family activities, from driving the kids to sport events to gathering family and friends around the table. Cooking a lovely meal for loved ones is one of Taurus's favorite pastimes.

TAURUS MOTHER

A Taurus mother is affectionate and protective and wants nothing but the best for her children. A Taurus mother will always be at the school play or sports fixture, no matter how busy she is. She thrives on routine and brings up her kids with boundaries, so they know just where they stand. They soon learn that when she says no, she means it. She wants her children to grow up to be responsible, self-assured, and confident adults.

TAURUS FATHER

A Taurus father will do everything he can to make his family as happy and stable as possible because he values family life so highly. Dependable and responsible, he works as many jobs as necessary to provide for his family to the best of his ability. He leads his family and guides them without being bossy or a nag. A Taurus man makes a great dad.

HEALTH AND WELLBEING

A sensuous sign, Taurus loves to be well, both physically and mentally. Exercise plays an important part in their lives because it makes them feel so good, but they are always ready to have a massage and relax after a hard workout. Taurus understands there is no point punishing yourself. As a result, Taurus is tough and rarely gets sick. At the first sign of illness, a Taurus knows to step back and nurture themselves.

It's not unusual for a Taurus to take a particular interest in alternative medicine, health foods, and exercise such as yoga. Keeping their mind healthy is as important as keeping their body well. Taurus carves out time to relax; they know that an afternoon spent chilling at home is as good for them as a night in a top restaurant, and they do both with relish. They love to sleep and need at least seven hours a night.

Food plays an important part in every Taurean life. Over-eating can become a problem, particularly as Taurus ages and their metabolic rate slows down. They need to remember to exercise; sometimes their hedonistic approach to life needs a bit of a kick start. Breaking out in a sweat a couple of times a week would help to no end.

Taurus rules the throat and neck. When they are feeling vulnerable or weak, a Taurus is more prone to catching the flu than other signs. Problems with their teeth are not unheard of, and Taurus should take special care and keep those dental appointments.

MONEY AND CAREERS

Taurus' reliable personality means that they are generally very good with money. They want a good job that pays well because they love all the nice things life has to offer. They spend freely and often on expensive ticket items but, in their defense, their spending is usually planned and never frivolous. They understand that it's important to put aside something for a rainy day because they want the security that comes with a nest egg.

In careers, Taurus excels at any career that needs persistence, reliability, and commitment. They can take abstract ideas and make them work, which means that any creative career, such as architecture or design, is a good fit with Taurus. They are not afraid to put in the hours to get the results, making them popular employees. They work well in laboratories and other environments where persistence is key. And while money is important to buy those luxuries they enjoy, they will not choose a career purely for the salary it pays. For those who work with a Taurus, it's easier if you accept that they know what they want and are unlikely to change their mind. But at least they will always stay cool in a crisis, making them an invaluable team member.

Taurus most likely won't choose to run their own business because they are happy to follow rules and not make their own. Plus, they like the routine and regularity of office hours – and the socializing!

GEMINI THE TWINS

MAY 21–JUNE 20

SNAPSHOT:

Element: Air

Quality: Mutability

Keyword: Versatility

Planetary Ruler: Mercury

Rules: Hand, arms, lung, nervous system

The first of the air signs, Gemini's job is to expand the horizons that Aries and Taurus have settled and cultivated. Always curious and adventurous, Gemini is ready to step into the unknown. Represented by the Twins, everything Gemini does has a built-in duality to it.

CHARACTER

Ruled by the planet Mercury, Gemini is known for its rational and intellectual approach to life. Quick-witted Gemini's mind is their most powerful tool as they navigate their way through the world. They are eternally questioning and motivated by the need to answer the question 'why?' Whether it's in the workplace or in their personal life, they have a burning desire to explore the world. Understanding and learning underscores everything they do. This is sometimes explained by the fact

that those born under Gemini feel something is missing; life is a quest to find their other half.

As a result, Gemini is engaged in an exhausting search for stimulation. They have so many interests, moving restlessly from one thing to the next in an instant. They are up-to-date with everything from the latest gossip to the latest tech. They love to know what's around the corner. However, Gemini is also the sign of the twins. At the heart of the Gemini is a duality. Often, they are at odds with themselves: what the heart demands, the mind rejects. This duality makes them quick-witted and impatient as they scour the world for entertainment and enlightenment. Along the way, they easily make friends and fill up their diaries to the point where the spontaneity they treasure can be hard to come by. But although they are always engaged and lively, their moods can change with the wind. Unlike some other signs, they are self-sufficient and easy to get along with.

THE DOWNSIDE

Sometimes, a Gemini is just too busy for their own good. They hate to be trapped in a routine or feel bored; the mutable air that marks their sign suggests this restless need for constant movement and diversion. They flit from one thing to the next, meaning they can easily become a hostage to their own hyperactivity. An inability to concentrate for any length of time means that Gemini can come across as superficial because they are so easily distracted. They are impatient and sometimes it can seem that the person they find the most interesting is themselves! But one advantage of this is that they never dwell on their troubles for any length of time. They move on quickly and adapt to change instantly.

As the sign of the twins, Gemini is often accused of being two-faced, but this is just a reflection of the inherent battle between the two sides of their sign. They don't mean to be that way; it's just the way they are.

LOVE

For a Gemini, love is all about the seduction of the mind. Unlike Taurus, they aren't motivated by the body's sensuousness; they are too busy with the rational exploration of their partner's mind. Once they're reassured that they have met their intellectual equal, Gemini will then think about their physical compatibility. Always ready to flirt, a Gemini might go through many different lovers until they find the 'one' who matches their intellect and energy. They want excitement, variety, and passion, and when they find the right person, their partner will not just be a lover, but also a friend who they can share everything with. Then, they will be faithful and will put the other person first.

Their endless questioning and curiosity can drive some people crazy, because they see Gemini as just plain interfering and nosy. Their rational approach can come across as fickle and unfeeling, but the motivation for a Gemini is to find their missing twin – the person who makes them whole. If you understand this, then Gemini can make a great partner and any obstacles miraculously melt away as the two become a whole.

Gemini's curiosity means that they are good listeners and so they find it very easy to start relationships, because who doesn't love being listened to? They pick up friends and lovers easily and, since they don't need too much attention lavished on them, they can make ideal partners for those who hate to feel claustrophobic. However, finding their match is tricky because they are so easily bored. Geminis are attracted to anyone who presents a challenge, and it isn't unusual for a Gemini to get involved in a lengthy on-off relationship because it suits their fickle nature. Their biggest challenge in love is to find a partner who not only matches them now, but who will match them in years to come. Growing old together is the biggest of all the challenges for a Gemini seeking love.

GEMINI WOMAN

Over the years, Gemini women will change until they grow into the person they were always meant to be. With a million interests and a million friends, a Gemini woman is often reluctant to commit to a relationship in her twenties. As she ages, she starts to understand herself and her needs better, so that by her fifties she truly knows who she is and what is important. For that reason, some Gemini women will marry at least twice. The person who appealed to her when she was younger might not be the person who can continue to stimulate her curious mind as she ages.

GEMINI MAN

Like a Gemini woman, a Gemini man is all about the mind. Quick-witted and a bit of an enigma, he isn't about to court you in the traditional way. He will, however, keep you on your toes. Just when you think you have got him worked out, he will surprise you and do something completely unexpected. That means life with him is never boring, and you will never lose interest.

FAMILY AND FRIENDS

Everyone wants to be friends with a Gemini because they want to be friends with you, particularly if you are as strong minded and as good a communicator as they are. Gemini is the social sign of the Zodiac.

Their fun-loving personality attracts people instantly. It's never boring hanging out with Geminis because they just love to talk and talk. Their boundless curiosity and readiness to try new things means that they meet all kinds of different and interesting people who become their friends. With a wide friendship circle, Geminis rush from person to person. Sometimes, it might feel as though Gemini is just a bit too busy to give a friend the space and attention they crave. One bit of advice for Geminis is to take a deep breath, stop talking and to listen to your friends. Get to really know them, not just on a superficial level, and you will find that friendship so much more rewarding.

Geminis value intellectual debate and they want friends who can match them. Communication is key. Geminis are known for the ability to talk and talk and talk, and they get on best with other signs that can communicate as well as they can such as the other air signs: Aquarius and Libra.

Family is very important to a Gemini parent and they will work hard to build a strong emotional bond with their children. They don't put the same demands on their kids as they do their partner, and they don't expect their kids to match the demanding standards they set their friends! In some respects, family life doesn't come naturally to the restless Gemini but because they love everything family stands for, Geminis will find a way to make it work, even if it does mean being in two places at once.

Having a Gemini as a family member is great if you are willing to give them the space they need to be themselves. They love their family and will put family duties and obligations first, no matter what demands are made on their time. They tend to get on well with their siblings and are drawn to other family members who share their personality traits. However, they live life in their own idiosyncratic way and will challenge rules where they see fit. This can pose problems in some family dynamics if they are constantly pushing against family rules and traditions.

GEMINI MOTHER

Full of energy, a Gemini mother always has something on the go. She rarely gets bored, and neither do her children because their mothers are so full of fun and creative ideas. She works hard to make sure that her children feel loved and are happy with life. Her relaxed approach means that the kids always have someone to confide in, and they often see their mother as a friend.

GEMINI FATHER

A Gemini father is fun to be around. He loves to spoil his children and sometimes can be a bit remiss at setting boundaries. Like a Gemini mother, he wants his kids to be his friends. He is rarely strict as life is too short, but this can be a problem because there are times when a parent has to parent.

HEALTH AND WELLBEING

Geminis love to exercise because they love to keep fit. Since they are easily bored, they need to do a variety of exercises – and they work out best when they work out with others. Just as with every other aspect of their life, exercise is an excuse to be sociable. The loneliness of a solitary run is not for them. They are much more likely – and will do better – if they belong to a running club. Loving the latest fad, a Gemini will be the first to try out the newest gym class and equipment. Variety is the spice of life for a Gemini. They are super competitive, but mostly with themselves. They set goals and expect to achieve them. Other people are there to keep them company. Their problem is sticking to their exercise routine. Boredom is never far away, so they just have to remember to mix it up. That way, they are more likely to stick with it.

Geminis are ruled by their lungs, hands, and arms. They can suffer from more than their fair share of coughs and colds and should be aware of that, especially in the winter months. They should also watch out for any symptoms of arthritis and take care of their hands, especially if they work a lot on computers and their phones. All their digital communication can give them a tendency towards carpal tunnel issues if they don't take care and make sure to take a break from all that technology!

MONEY AND CAREERS

Gemini and work is a match made in heaven. Adaptable and logical, Geminis pick up information very quickly; they easily absorb facts and apply them with lightning speed. The downside is that because anything and everything interests them, and they pick up things so quickly, they get bored very fast. Geminis need constant mental stimulation and a buzzy working environment with lots of interesting colleagues to thrive. Working in any kind of repetitive job won't work for them.

A life-long love of words means that many Geminis find careers in education and writing, possibly as a journalist, or any social media set-up. Blogging would be a perfect fit for a Gemini. While their skill with words is undoubtedly great, writing their masterpiece alone in their attic might be a step too far for some Geminis. They would rather be out there networking and making contacts; as such any kind of business would suit their entrepreneurial flair so long as it involved other people in some capacity.

Money doesn't particularly motivate Geminis and they aren't the best at handling their finances. They do like spending money on the things they enjoy doing such as traveling, reading, and any kind of cultural event. Their split personality means it's quite easy for a Gemini to spend impulsively, and to avoid this they need to set financial goals and then stick to them. The duality of Gemini means that for every Gemini who is a spendthrift, there's another who hates to part with their cash.

CANCER THE CRAB

JUNE 21–JULY 22

SNAPSHOT

Element: Water

Quality: Cardinal

Keywords: Nurturing

Planetary Ruler: Moon

Rules: Stomach, digestive system, breasts

The first of the water signs, Cancer is depicted as a
Crab for good reason. Highly sensitive and vulnerable,
Cancer's tough outer shell defends them from everything
life throws at them.

CHARACTER

What a paradox Cancer is! Their loyalty, emotional sensitivity, and
intuition are matched only by their insecurity and readiness to
attack if they feel at all threatened. At first sight, the Crab can come
across as cold and distant but over time, once they trust you, Cancer
will reveal their gentle nature, genuine compassion, and almost
mystical capabilities. Cancer is a contradictory sign because it is
both a water and cardinal sign. The water sign gives Cancer their
emotional sensitivity, their imagination, their intuition, and their

kindness. The cardinal element brings with it a steely determination and tough inner core that makes Cancer unexpectedly ambitious and enterprising. Perhaps their paradoxical nature is best summed up by the fact that while they are invariably kind and gentle, they can become instantly nasty and vindictive when crossed.

Another result of the cardinal/water combination is Cancer's uncanny intuition. They can read people and situations better than any other sign; they seem to know what you're thinking before you do, and this can make them over-sensitive as they pester you to find out if what was on your mind is what they thought it was. They won't rest until they know and if you don't tell them, they will almost certainly sulk, because Cancer is prone to bouts of moodiness. Cancer is ruled by the moon, which has a direct impact on their moods, which wax and wane as swiftly and powerfully as Earth's satellite.

Cancer is incredibly loyal; they will remember birthdays not just of their friends but also of their friends' mothers. They also are nostalgic and sentimental. Throwing away old birthday cards is almost impossible for Cancer. They hang on to everything.

Their ambitious streak means they set themselves far-reaching goals, which they then go after with a determination few can match.

THE DOWNSIDE

Like the crab, Cancer will readily retreat into their shell if they feel at all threatened. They hate confrontation and do their best to avoid it at all times. Just like a crab, they avoid direct conflict; they are more likely to lash out in a passive-aggressive way. Emotions often hold Cancer to ransom. At times, they can allow their fears to overwhelm them so that they lose focus and are unable to act or think straight. Their moods can change from moment to moment; one minute they are laughing hysterically, the next they are sobbing.

They tend to be too possessive and demanding of others, and because they have a terrible fear of being abandoned, they often hang on to friends well past their sell-by date. It also means that sometimes they come over as being a bit too controlling. If you can convince a Cancer to be open and say what's on their mind without them feeling threatened, you will build trust and, when they conquer their innate insecurity, life is a lot easier – not just for them – but for those closest to them.

LOVE

Cancer falls in love quickly and dramatically! They are quick to commit and once they are in a relationship, they will try their hardest to make sure it works. It takes a lot for them to admit a relationship might not be working.

When things are going well, Cancer will do anything for their beloved. They will go that extra mile to defend them and to make sure they are okay. Their sensitive nature means that they become very sentimental when things are going well, showering their partner with tokens of love. When things start to go badly, they get hurt quickly. For that reason, they are careful not to show just how vulnerable they are when they start a love affair. Yet when handled with care and respect they blossom, giving devotion and loyalty for life.

Cancer will keep every token – tickets, cards, and gifts – anything that reminds them of the relationship. They notice things that other signs just never pick up, and they remember. For Cancer, memories and tokens are links to their loved one and provide a constant reminder of what they have. They don't see it as slightly obsessive hoarding!

Love is always serious for Cancer; they prize respect and devotion and want nothing more than a partner who reciprocates their feelings. Because they are so easy to talk to and sensitive, it makes them attractive to others and they generally have no problem meeting people. Their sensitivity gives them an air of vulnerability and makes you want to protect them. Cancer enjoys being looked after and they very much enjoy looking after their partner. They don't mind changing their behavior to make sure their partner is happy, and the relationship survives. Once they are in a committed relationship, there's nothing they would not do for their partner. They love marking the special moments they share with their partner and their fantastic memory means that they will remember not just that first kiss but the first time they did anything together as a couple – and they will have a memento of the occasion!

As a result, it sets the bar quite high for how a relationship with a Cancerian should function. It will take some time to really get to know what makes Cancer tick; they hide their vulnerabilities early in relationships to protect themselves and only come out of their shell once they feel confident. Their sensitivity means that their feelings can be easily hurt. A jilted Cancer will be temporarily floored. However, that feeling does not last too long; once they have processed their feelings, they pick themselves up and move on.

CANCER WOMAN

Despite appearing enigmatic, Cancer women are actually surprisingly insecure. They seem to not want to be pinned down and so can appear moody and elusive at first, making it hard to know what they think of you. Once you have won their trust, they are totally committed and will lavish love and attention on their chosen one with half an eye on a shared future of domestic bliss.

CANCER MAN

Cancer men can be hard to work out. Sometimes, they are over-attentive, lavishing you with flowers and romantic dinners. Other times, they seem aloof and inconsiderate. That's because they like their personal space and retreat if they feel it is being infringed. Give them space and everything will be fine.

FAMILY AND FRIENDS

Family and friends are what make Cancer tick. They attract friends and lovers because they are loyal, more than willing to commit, and emotionally very sophisticated. Home is what really matters to Cancer, and they expect those closest to them to love home as much as they do. Nothing is more important to a Cancer than their family and friends.

Cancer is the most maternal of all the signs and that includes the men. They love children and they love nurturing a family environment. As well as creating their own family, the family Cancer is born into plays a central role – for good and bad – throughout their life. But it's not just family that matters. Cancer is devoted to their friends; they will go that extra mile to keep in touch with their large circle of friends by frequently texting and calling. When they can, they love to get people together and often host parties and dinners just for the pleasure of seeing their friends together. They make fantastic hosts because they love to cook at home for their loved ones. Gathering people around the table to eat their homemade food is about as good as it gets for Cancer.

No other Zodiac sign is as loyal as Cancer. They will do anything, literally, to protect anyone they love, and, in return, they expect the same level of devotion. If that suits, then any friendship will last a lifetime. If it doesn't, be warned. Cancer will not understand your need for privacy and space. They want to be your friend 24/7.

With family, they show the same level of devotion, which works well for their children and for their partners when things are going well.

Ever nurturing, creating a home is so important to Cancer because it is a place of safety and refuge, a bit like the shell of the crab. It is where they can enjoy family time. Domestic bliss was made for the Cancer, who will do all in their power to smooth the waters and make sure that everyone has what they need and is getting along. This is facilitated by their powers of intuition and their sensitivity. They tend to be overprotective as a parent but that's because they love their children so much. If they have pets, they lavish the same love and attention on their animals. They can't help it.

CANCER MOTHER

Motherhood was meant for a Cancer woman. She loves her children and her home unconditionally, and will do everything in her power to make sure her kids feel nurtured, loved, and wanted at all times. Nothing is too much trouble and she will do anything and everything for her loved ones. Sometimes, she needs to step back and allow them a bit of independence.

CANCER FATHER

Like his female counterpart, a Cancer man builds his world around his family. He wants to be the best dad ever and will pull out all the stops to make it happen. More than any other sign, he will go out of his way to be there for his children. It's not just a question of providing for them, he wants to be emotionally and physically present as much as he can be.

HEALTH AND WELLBEING

Cancerians tend to put on weight as they age, so they have to make sure they keep up a regular exercise regime and don't overeat. For Cancer, exercise serves a dual purpose. It not only helps keep weight off, but it also helps to balance and calm Cancer's highly emotional state of

mind. The best exercises for Cancer are ones that combine mind and body, such as yoga or Pilates. That's because they see exercise as being as much about the spirit as the body, and for that reason, noisy cardio classes aren't really for them.

Cancer rules the digestive system. Their sensitive nature and tendency to worry about things means that they often suffer from upset stomachs caused by stress and other external factors. Their emotions are played out in their stomachs. As a result, it is best to avoid very rich and spicy foods because they can add to the stress the stomach is already under. Blander food such as oats and rice will calm and soothe the Cancer's sensitive stomach.

They are also known to over-indulge – as are all the water signs – and will reach for that extra glass of wine or a pudding when they are already full. They need to try to limit such over-indulgence to special occasions and one-off treats. By doing so, their stomach will thank them in the long run.

It is not surprising, given the strong connection between Cancer and family that the sign also rules the stomach and breasts. They are both connected with motherhood, fertility, and nurturing, of which Cancer is a master.

MONEY AND CAREERS

Cancer loves everything to do with the home and domestic life but that does not mean they expect to stay at home. Their sensitive, thoughtful nature means that they work best when they are surrounded by other people, particularly in the many caring professions that work for them from medicine to therapy. Also, their natural leadership skills mean they work well in any environment that needs a sensitive and empathetic leader. They willingly take the initiative and are happy to work hard. Their determination and ambition mean that they set themselves high goals, but they will never exploit people on their way to the top. Instead, they look to help others on their career paths, just as they have been helped on their way to the top. They are organized and energetic, which makes them a great coworker.

As a boss, a Cancer will be a bit like your parent. For them, work is another family environment and when it works, a Cancer-led team is a magnificent thing. If a Cancer feels, however, that their team members are not loyal or trustworthy, they will soon let their feelings be known.

Money for Cancer means security. It is the shell that protects them. It is important for them to have a nest egg, and they work hard to make sure that they can save as they go along. Others might perceive Cancers as being mean when they are, in fact, very careful with their money so that they have enough for the things that really matter to them, such as their family and friends.

LEO THE LION

JULY 23–AUGUST 22

SNAPSHOT

Element: Fire

Quality: Fixed

Keywords: Action, power

Planetary Ruler: Sun

Rules: Heart, back, and spinal cord

The second fire sign belongs to the king or queen of the jungle, Leo the golden Lion, bathed in the sun's rays. Leo loves to be the center of attention at all times. A consummate performer, what you see is what you get, but Leos are much more complex than they first appear.

CHARACTER

A typical Leo is royalty personified; they are confident and loyal to the many admirers who have earned the right to be their friend. Smart and exuding self-confidence, Leo is spontaneous and fun-loving. Life for them is for not just living, but for getting as much as possible out of it. They pack every day with activities and people, making sure that they are center stage at all times, because Leos crave the adulation that comes with being center stage. But they don't just want people to pay homage to them – it matters very much to them that their friends like what they like and think the way Leos think. For them, that's proof of another person's loyalty, which they set great store by. Being in charge comes naturally to Leo and they certainly don't expect anyone to tell them what to do or to challenge their authority. If that all sounds a bit bossy, it is, but Leo brings such charm and optimism that nobody minds. Their busy social calendar attests to the popularity of Leo. That's because they are generous and compassionate, especially if you are one of their admirers. For those who follow the call of Leo and pay homage to them, the rewards can be great.

THE DOWNSIDE

The downside of Leo is pretty much the upside. It's how you view them. The sense of entitlement that comes with their readiness to lead can come across as overbearing and arrogant. Similarly, their love of the limelight makes them seem vain and self-centered. Life is never dull around a Leo, but sometimes there can be just a bit too much drama.

Sometimes it is hard to remember that a lot of Leo's behavior is, in fact, a very clever act. They don't want anybody to see how hard they try or how vulnerable they often feel. In an effort to keep themselves at the center of everything, they sometimes exaggerate and are not averse to painting themselves in a favorable light to the detriment of others. They don't really see that as showing off or boasting; it is just a question of others seeing them as the special person they believe they are.

An idealist, Leo believes they alone have the answer to what makes a great life and they are determined to share that with others. They have an opinion on literally everything and are not slow in giving it and advising others, even when they have not asked for it. Unfortunately for Leo and for everyone else, they will never willingly admit having made a mistake and that can lead to accusations of controlling and demanding behavior. If they can just step back and relax, Leo's loving and warm personality will get the chance to shine.

LOVE

Leo's apparent self-confidence and easy-going manner make it easy for them to attract people and that means they have no shortage of romantic partners. When they are in a relationship, Leos put the L into love. Romance was made for them! They love everything about being in love from the long calls and soppy messages, to romantic walks, and cozy dinners *à deux*, basically every cliché that was ever written about romance. That means that when things are good in a relationship with a Leo they are fantastic. A Leo will be passionate, committed, and thrilled by their partner's every move. However, when things go wrong, they can go spectacularly wrong for a Leo. Jealousy and possessiveness soon reveal the ugly side of Leo and the controlling and demanding side of Leo's personality can appear. High maintenance is one way of describing a Leo. But in exchange for that they will throw themselves wholeheartedly into a relationship they find exciting and challenging. As a result, anyone who has been in a relationship with a Leo will never forget it once it's over. Their generosity and excitement are hard to beat, and that's why it can be so hard to let a Leo go.

Perhaps surprisingly, given Leo's tough exterior, they are easily wounded and are very vulnerable when a relationship does go wrong. However, you might not suspect any of this, as Leos don't like to show any of this once a relationship ends. Don't be taken in by that cold exterior. Inside, Leo does have a soft side and feels rejection as keenly as the next person.

LEO WOMAN

A Leo woman loves all the romance that goes with a romance. She wants to be given flowers and taken out for candlelit dinners and to spend her Saturday nights with her partner. Her ideas might be a little conventional, but if you try and deviate from them she will soon let you know her discontent. Similarly, it is hard for her to keep up the pretense once her passion fades. If it's over, as far as she is concerned, it's over and there's no point pretending otherwise. She wants order in her relationship, but it will be the order she has specified and not yours. Get the rules right and a relationship with a Leo woman can be highly rewarding.

LEO MAN

The king of the jungle, a Leo man likes to be in charge. Allow him to keep center stage and all will be well in any relationship. Leo is always fun company, wants everyone to have a great time, and will work hard to make sure they do. But, if you make the mistake of telling him what to do, it will all fall apart quickly. Get used to sharing Leo with other people because he likes to have his friends around at all times. But if you are the chosen one, he will commit to you and he will mean it.

FAMILY AND FRIENDS

When it comes to family, Leo will always be loyal. They will never shun their families and will do everything to protect them, but although you would never know it they are not real homebodies. For them, their role is to protect and help their family and while they are incredibly proud of their family, they remain, at heart, too independent. In their family, they will lead and expect their family to follow. This can lead to family disagreements when their authority is challenged. If a brother or sister is a Leo, it can make for tricky family dynamics as they try to impose their will on their siblings and parents. However, their investment in their family means that they can always be trusted to help out whenever called upon.

Similarly, Leo makes a great and loyal friend, as long as it is on their terms. They love to be surrounded by people and are incredibly hospitable. Hosting parties is second nature to a Leo. You will always be welcomed at a Leo's home provided you observe the unwritten rule that they take center stage and you do not try to upstage them! Anyone who does that will soon be sent packing. Leo's belief that they have

the answers to life's questions can make them frustrating friends at times, because they are always ready to offer advice or an opinion even when it has not been sought. The other side of the coin is that Leo is honest and has great integrity. Their spontaneous nature responds to small children, whether they are their own or not, and they will always include kids in their plans.

Leos are smart people and they like to surround themselves with their intellectual equals. Time spent with a Leo will never be boring; they will challenge you and will enjoy lively debates and questions.

LEO MOTHER

Full of energy and affection, a Leo mother thinks her children are the greatest kids ever. She wants them to be the best at everything and will go out of her way to make sure they have everything they need to achieve that. She's always on the sideline cheering them on and in the front row of every school play, and she'll be shouting or clapping the loudest, so you know she's there. She can be very strict and demanding, and her kids need to know how to deal with her.

LEO FATHER

A Leo father is as ambitious for his children as he is for himself. He relishes the role of a father because it brings out his protective streak and his authoritative tendencies. After all, if his children don't do as he says, who will? That doesn't mean that he isn't fun to be around. He is, and he will do his best to give his children a happy and fun childhood. Full of energy, he will encourage his kids to try anything and everything.

HEALTH AND WELLBEING

Ruled by the heart, Leo's emotional wellbeing is often reflected in their physical wellbeing. When things get too much for them emotionally, they retreat to their beds with a high fever, claiming nothing is wrong, just a bug they can't shake.

To try and keep on top of their general wellbeing, Leos love to exercise. Like Gemini, a solitary run is not for them. They like to see and be seen at the gym. Always the first to try the latest fitness craze and invariably wearing the latest gear, they wholeheartedly embrace exercise. Their competitive side means that it's not just about keeping well, but also about being the fittest and fastest. One of the downsides of this, is that some Leos might take shortcuts to achieve the results they are after.

With their endless stamina and determination, it can be hard for a Leo to know when to stop and they are prone to injury from just going too far; they need to make sure they keep an eye on their back because Leo rules the spinal cord and it's one of their weak spots. On the positive side, when Leo is injured, they recover quickly because their energy levels are generally so high.

Emotionally, Leos need to remember it is not a sign of weakness to admit that, at times, things are hard and that they, like everyone else, might fail or face disappointment. By opening up and admitting their true feelings, Leo can live a much more rewarding life.

MONEY AND CAREERS

Leos are workaholics. Extremely ambitious, they will work every hour needed, which might surprise some people. Since their love of the limelight is well known, people mistakenly assume this means that the typical Leo is lazy. Nothing could be further from the truth. They are very skilful delegators who know how to get the best out of people.

They will take risks in business and are happiest in control of their empire whether it is as a chief executive or just sitting at the kitchen

table working on a start-up. If they hire people, the smart ones know that to keep on their good side, they have to work hard and show due deference. Then there is no stopping how much a Leo will help them. The more contact a Leo has with people and the more they are put in the heart of things, the more they thrive. Leos are natural-born performers, whether it is on the stage or in front of a class of fifth graders. It's all attention, and that's oxygen to a Leo.

Their willingness to take risks means they make money. Money allows them to buy just what they want to make their lives content. If they don't have the money, they will put it on their credit card. Debt doesn't worry a Leo because they assume they will earn the money to pay it off. Life is for living now, and there is little point in saving for a rainy day that may never come.

VIRGO THE VIRGIN

AUGUST 23–SEPTEMBER 22

SNAPSHOT

Element: Earth

Quality: Mutable

Keywords: Order, detail, dedication

Planetary Ruler: Mercury

Rules: Intestines, abdomen, female reproductive system

With a keen eye for detail and a supreme ability for analysis and criticism, the second of the earth signs, Virgo the Virgin, can sometimes make their lives too difficult by over-thinking and judging everything. Duty figures highly for Virgos and work features significantly in their life.

CHARACTER

Virgo's keen intellect coupled with the ability to over-analyze means that they have a perfectionist streak that few other signs can hope to match. Their clarity of mind coupled with an ability to concentrate and learn means that Virgos are continually looking to expand their knowledge, not just because they have to, for work, for example, but also because

they truly enjoy learning. Self improvement in every and any aspect of life is what makes a Virgo tick. There is so much to know and only so much time to learn it all.

Along with their extraordinary capacity for industry – like the other earth signs Capricorn and Taurus – they have the great gift of insight, which makes them extremely capable at almost anything they turn their hand to. Articulate, thanks to Mercury, Virgos are great communicators and their power of observation means little goes unnoticed. They love beauty and make sure that they surround themselves with beautiful things, be it the clothes they wear or how they decorate their homes. It doesn't have to be expensive, but it will always be tasteful and attractive because that is all Virgos know.

Idealists, Virgos will push not only themselves but others. Their to-do list is always long because, well, there is so much they want to accomplish. Determination and hard work mean that they will work through that list whatever anybody else says. At the same time, they willingly help others and sometimes this willingness to put others first can turn them into a bit of a martyr, because they hate the idea that they might disappoint.

DOWNSIDE

A never-ending quest for perfection means that Virgo can be overly critical, not just of themselves, but of those around them. But if you think a Virgo can be harsh on you, they are a million times harsher on themselves. Their desire for perfection can lead to nagging and criticism because they are on an eternal quest for an impossible ideal. This can also come across as being overly demanding and can put people's backs up. When others cannot see the perfection a Virgo seeks and they settle for second best, it infuriates a typical Virgo, who then retreats into sulky martyrdom. If Virgo could only lighten up with the impossibly high standards they set themselves, then everything else would flow naturally from there – and life would be a bit more relaxing for everyone.

Born worriers, Virgos don't just worry about the things they can control but also about everything else, from climate change to concern about the wellbeing of complete strangers. Anything can make Virgo worry. This all fits in with their search for perfection. In a perfect world, there would be no need to worry.

LOVE

The Virgin might symbolize Virgo but don't let that deceive you, they are some of the best lovers in the Zodiac. That's if you pass muster. Virgo's high standards mean they are very choosy about their partners. Their standards are so high it can be hard for anyone to make the grade. They would rather be alone than compromise, but if they can be realistic, love can be long lasting and rewarding.

A first date with a Virgo can be intimidating. They are looking for an immediate connection, intellectual stimulation, and physical attraction. Most people won't make it past the first date, but it does provide a great time-saver if nothing else! The problem is that Virgos apply the same high standards they apply to themselves to everyone else. Not much gets past a Virgo. A wise Virgo will recognize this and will cut the other person a bit of slack.

Despite their intelligence and critical thinking, a Virgo likes nothing more than to be swept off their feet. They want to be wooed. Romance – the flowers, the candlelit dinners, the long walks, the lazy days in bed – all matter to a Virgo. As well as sweeping them off their feet, a suitor has to pass a rigorous checklist of an ideal partner. You have to be clean, loyal, respectful, and intelligent. Flings don't hold much appeal for Virgos; they waste time. What they want is a long-term partner who fits in with their family and who will eventually be a great parent if they decide to have children.

Meanwhile, they want their partner to need them, but they shouldn't be too needy. What's more, Virgos are driven to try and fix anything that ails their partner. They forget sometimes that they are in a

romantic relationship and not in a counseling session. Somewhat perversely, Virgos's approach to intimacy can be either all or nothing. They might choose to keep secrets, making it hard for a partner to get close, or they bombard their partner with so much personal information so quickly, they up and run. The best course would be for Virgo to take a deep breath before spilling the beans.

Virgos should remember that relationships are a two-way street. In order to have a successful partnership, they might have to let down their guard and rely on their partner. Remember, any partner will have passed stringent tests, and by letting down their guard, Virgo can lay the groundwork for a long-lasting love relationship based on respect and some give and take.

VIRGO WOMAN

With a tendency to fret and take things too seriously, a Virgo woman sets great store by mental attraction when seeking her partner. She loves to share intellectual things in life such as books, and wants a partner who enjoys them as much as her.

VIRGO MAN

Just like a Virgo woman, a Virgo man can take himself too seriously in relationships. He can be too hard on himself and on his partner. If he lightens up, then life is much better all around.

FAMILY AND FRIENDS

Virgo's rich inner life means that they can come across as being self-contained and shy, and while it's true that they are reserved until they know you, once you earn a Virgo's trust, they are your friend for life. They take friendship very seriously indeed. With their families, it is a different matter because they are family and so what matters is giving them their all.

Virgos make great friends and family members despite their unavoidable tendency to be critical. That's because their sense of duty will always win out over their critical tendencies. A Virgo will be the first to offer help and will never shirk their responsibilities. They will always remember birthdays and if you are in trouble, they will drop everything and run over to help. Nothing is too much trouble for a Virgo; whether it's washing the dishes after dinner or taking care of elderly relatives, a Virgo will do it willingly.

They show a similar devotion to their family. The wellbeing and happiness of those closest to them is of upmost importance to a Virgo. But they are more likely to show their love through their actions than through words. Action comes much more easily to a Virgo than verbal expressions. Having said that, Virgo's perception and critical abilities mean that they can offer insights and advice on a day-to-day basis. Friends and family, alike, come to rely on Virgo for their impartial advice and their problem-solving.

Often, Virgos can be shy, and they do not make the first move when they meet new people. They are weighing up the person before deciding whether to invest in their friendship or not. When they do, a Virgo is invariably gentle and kind to their friends. As a result, they are very popular. Ironically, Virgos often feel they don't do enough for their friends when, in fact, they do go that extra mile. They will readily do things which other signs of the Zodiac think are a step too far. Friendships with a Virgo will last a lifetime, particularly if they find friends who are happy to give back as much as Virgo gives. A Virgo much prefers an evening with a few good friends to a huge party. They don't need a packed calendar to be happy, and are just as happy with a quiet night in as a night out on the town.

VIRGO MOTHER

A perfectionist, a Virgo mother will want her children to be the best they can be, and she can find it hard to let her kids find their own way, although she prizes independence above everything else. Rational and low-key, she's very practical and the family's backbone. She is the one who organizes her family and thinks through everything down to the last detail. She always puts her family first.

VIRGO FATHER

A Virgo father likes everything to be organized down to the last detail and, like a Virgo mother, he will work hard towards the greater good of the family. Always on the move, he keeps his family entertained so they never know what the next challenge will be. Sometimes his family might find his need for perfection just a tad irritating.

HEALTH AND WELLBEING

Virgo rules the stomach, which means that Virgos can suffer from all kinds of stomach problems. That's because they are born worriers and control freaks! Their need to control does sometimes mean they are more likely to get indigestion and stomach ulcers. Before any big event, Virgos often get an upset stomach; their emotional state is always reflected in their physical state. As a result, a Virgo knows to always trust their gut instinct. When they do, they invariably avoid difficult situations. To avoid problems with their stomachs, a Virgo should avoid over-processed snacks, too much caffeine, and stick to a diet of fresh, healthy, and not over-spiced foods.

Exercise is a life-saver for a Virgo. They like all kinds of exercise but have a weakness for trying out the latest gym-based exercise. But being a Virgo, a big, busy class is not for them. They prefer those expensive, design-led fashionable classes where everyone wears the latest gear.

They like to make a good impression at any class they take. Virgo's love of exercise knows no bounds. It is easy for a Virgo to become obsessive as they don't know when to stop! Ever the hypochondriac, Virgo can obsess over every twinge. Taking time out to do some stress-relieving classes, such as meditation, would help Virgo to relax. Relaxation techniques and meditation would help a Virgo to still their racing mind and help them with their tendency to overthink and criticize. Taking their foot off that particular pedal would help give them a better life balance.

MONEY AND CAREERS

Virgo's love of detail means that they want their work to be perfect. As such, they make a great member of any work team. Able to juggle a lot of detail and multi-task, and with fabulous organisational abilities, they excel at any job that requires analytical skills. Excellent communicators and happy to speak in public, they are well suited to any job that requires them to interface with others.

The downside for a Virgo is that they are so capable they can find themselves a bit too much in demand. Their bosses can see that a Virgo will get the job done quicker and more thoroughly than almost any other sign. As such, they can find themselves stuck in the office or running after-school clubs because they can't say no to any new challenge. That means they never get home quite when they want to. Unlike other signs, Virgos make great employees, although once they start to feel a little taken advantage of, they will start to dream of the day they run their own business and will work to reach that goal. That's their employer's loss!

Virgo's sensible streak extends to how they manage their money. They spend if they think it's necessary and on things that are important to them. They will think twice before buying anything expensive but if they can justify it, they will buy it. If it's not going to give them the cost benefit they expect, they'll save their money. For them, money is all about enjoying life and buying the things that make life a bit special.

LIBRA THE SCALES

SEPTEMBER 23–OCTOBER 22

SNAPSHOT

Element: Air

Quality: Cardinal

Keywords: Balance

Planetary Ruler: Venus

Rules: Lower back and diaphragm

Libra is the only one of the twelve Zodiac signs to be represented by a physical object – a set of scales – rather than a living creature. It means that a typical Libra will seek balance in every aspect of their life. The first day of Libra occurs during the autumn equinox, when night and day are perfectly balanced.

CHARACTER

The second of the air signs, Libra is the most charming of the three. Their love of balance means that they try, at all times, to keep things harmonious. Chaos horrifies a Libra. They want their surroundings and their life to be orderly and serene and work hard to achieve that. At the same time, they are clever and charming. Able to keep things at a distance, they are great company.

Natural-born mediators and great diplomats, they try to act fairly at all times. The scales mean that Librans are always going to look at both sides of any argument. They try to avoid jumping to conclusions before they have looked at every angle. This can sometimes come across as their being deliberately provocative. They are not; they are being thoughtful and thorough.

Venus rules Libra and brings with it a love of beauty. Being surrounded by beauty and beautiful objects is extremely important to a Libra. They know how to indulge themselves and need little excuse to do so. Their innate serenity means they love music and art, and their witty conversation means they are highly sought-after as friends and lovers. This love of all things beautiful means that they want everything they do and every experience they have to be one hundred percent perfect. Their view is: 'Why bother if it is less than perfect?' Such idealism can be hard to maintain on a daily basis.

DOWNSIDE

Perhaps one of the surprising things about a typical Libra is that despite their outward appearance of elegance and serenity, inside they can lack self-confidence, which is made worse by their tendency to worry. They are incredibly tough on themselves and are always their own harshest critic. Libras want others to think well of them and will go out of their way to please others to their own detriment. Despite their ability to listen and empathize, it is too easy for Libra's opinions and desires to get sublimated to those of their companions. If only they could have more confidence in their own opinions and values.

Librans hate to see people argue and yet they can often be the source of disagreements, despite their reputation for balance. The fact is that finding and keeping a balanced life is actually much more difficult for a Libra than it might appear. The effort of diplomacy can lead a Libra to paralysis. They find that decision-making one way or another is too hard, and they work themselves into a frenzy considering all the pros

and cons. Sometimes, they should just go with the flow and go easy on themselves and others. Not every decision is life-changing and not every decision requires them to compare and contrast. Sometimes the answer is blindingly clear, and they should just follow their instinct.

LOVE

Ruled by Venus, Libra is a contradiction. On one hand, relationships are vitally important; they are what make a Libra tick. With a partner's strength to fill in their weaker aspects, they feel that balance is restored. On the other hand, Libra is ruled by the head and not the heart, so it is hard for a Libra to plunge into a relationship without thinking through all the pros and cons. Their dislike of drama means that they take a while to commit and they keep their distance to protect themselves from conflict and emotional upheaval. This ambivalence can come across as a lack of interest, which is far from the truth. The reality is that Libras are romantics. They might think they like to be alone but in reality, they don't. They want to love and be loved. They want a special person to be with them always.

A Libra will put your happiness above their own; they will want to make you happy whatever the personal costs. So, they won't pick a fight. Instead, since they are always looking for the balance in any situation, they will try and work things out. That means they might pretend things are good when they are not because, they reason, eventually problems can be ironed out. When a relationship does fold, they will try and move on without resorting to name calling or anything quite so low; they will always remember the best about you.

Ever the romantic, Libra wants to believe in the happy ever after. Having finally made up their mind to commit, they will become a loyal, loving and generous partner whose trust is guaranteed. If you want somebody to continually challenge you, then perhaps Libra is the wrong choice, because they always say yes to the ones they love.

For their part, Libra is looking for somebody who has the intelligence, elegance, energy, manners, and that certain *je ne sais quoi* to satisfy them.

LIBRA WOMAN

A Libra woman loves to flirt and will go all out to win her partner. Candlelit dinners, fresh flowers, and romantic music are all part of her armor. She will lavish all her time and attention on her partner so that they feel truly chosen and special. In bed, she is an attentive lover.

LIBRA MAN

Just like female Libra, a Libra man wants company and works better as part of a team. Once he commits, he's loyal and devoted and looks to make the relationship as perfect as it can be. He will, however, want to keep his individuality at all times – it's all a question of balance.

FAMILY AND FRIENDS

Libra is a social being. They love nothing more than being surrounded by friends and family. By putting fairness at the heart of everything they do, Libra is one of the easiest of all the signs to get along with. People are drawn to them because they exude calm and grace. It doesn't take long to realize that once you have made a Libran friend, that friendship will be of central importance and will most likely last a lifetime. Libra know they function better around other people and so make sure their friends feel valued. Always willing to compromise for the greater good, Libra can see the bigger picture in any situation, which makes for a smooth ride.

Libra loves a good party, but one word of caution. For all their seemingly outgoing behavior and sociability, Libra also needs some time alone to recalibrate and recharge so that they can then throw themselves back into the social whirl. Libra is so sensitive to others' needs – that's what makes them so attractive – that they run the risk of not meeting their own needs. They are also sensitive to how others perceive them and take personally every slight and every perceived injustice, which can lead them to retreat into their shells and give the impression of being standoffish.

Family plays a pivotal role in Libra's life. They love nothing more than gathering together their nearest and dearest on a regular basis. They have a natural ability to create a peaceful and harmonious atmosphere, which is irresistible when combined with their charm. When people do fall out, Libra can be guaranteed to act as the mediators and peacemakers. Their energy inspires others and they are often the last to leave any party.

LIBRA MOTHER

Nothing is too much trouble for a Libra mother who wants to make sure that her children have the best of everything. She understands just how precious childhood is and wants to be part of her child's life for as long as possible. The Libra knack for attracting beauty and surrounding themselves with beautiful objects creates a harmonious environment for the family. Libra is reluctant to waste money but will use what she has creatively to make the perfect atmosphere.

LIBRA FATHER

A Libra father waits patiently for the moment when his children can become his friends. Before then, he will be patient and kind and while he knows that discipline is part of growing up, he will make sure he is fair in all his dealings with his offspring. He, too, likes the good things in life and loves to share. He will give his children a great deal of freedom, but only once he knows that they have the ability to be sensible and independent.

HEALTH AND WELLBEING

The life-long quest for balance extends itself to how Libra views their health and wellbeing. Back problems can plague Libra and they don't like to suffer, so will do anything to get better. Libra are often susceptible to vague pains in their lower backs, kidneys and ovaries. Sometimes, these aches are as much about the Libra mind as a physical pain. Because they struggle to make up their minds they exist in a state of constant indecision, which can manifest itself in hard-to-define aches and pains.

Their remedy for this is to try and get better as quickly as possible. Short-term fixes can cause Libra all kinds of short-term problems. Lacking energy? A Libra will reach for a double espresso with extra sugar and then wonder why they feel lousy soon after!

It is important to their wellbeing that Libra incorporates physical exercise into their daily routine. It doesn't matter what they do, as long as they do something, although yoga is a great Libran exercise because it incorporates the balance between mind and body.

Normally well-balanced, Librans rarely express anger. They would rather work through their issues but, if they do lose their temper, then everyone knows about it! Any outburst is short-lived and causes Libra as much anguish as the recipient of their anger. For that reason, they try to avoid getting into situations where they might lose their rag.

MONEY AND CAREERS

Work is not a priority for most Librans, still less money. They are so much more interested in the world and all its possibilities that, for them, work should be about more than just earning a living. They want to do something that stimulates them intellectually and socially. Any job in the arts is attractive to Libra; their artistic sensibility lends itself to visual careers from photography to fashion design, interior design, and even computer design.

Another career that would seem to be a natural fit with a Libra is the law. Because of their understanding of the need to see both sides of an argument, they make good judges. Similarly, their powers of diplomacy and negotiation lend themselves to any career where those skills are required.

While money might not motivate the choice of a Libran career, Librans know what they are worth, and they won't hold back in asking for what they see as the appropriate pay. Although the finer things in life don't come cheap, Librans are not profligate. They know when to save and when to splurge and, as such, make their money go a long way.

Whatever Libra spend their days doing, they prefer to do it with other people. Working on their own is hard. They prefer face-to-face contact with other people at some point in the working day. However, for Libra work often doesn't feel like work. Every day they are learning something new and Libra values that as part of life's rich tapestry.

SCORPIO THE SCORPION

OCTOBER 23–NOVEMBER 21

SNAPSHOT

Element: Water

Quality: Fixed

Keywords: Regeneration, transformation

Planetary Ruler: Mars and Pluto

Rules: Sexual organs, rectum, reproductive organs

The second water sign and the eighth sign in the Zodiac, Scorpio is a complex sign that beautifully captures the idea of 'still waters running deep.' Intensity is the key to Scorpio. Ruled by the planet Pluto – the planet of transformation – they live life to the extreme and on their terms.

CHARACTER

Scorpio's symbol is the Scorpion for good reason. Much like a scorpion, which kills itself rather than be killed, Scorpios are in control of their destiny. Just as a scorpion can lose its tail and grow another one, Scorpios are able to reinvent themselves at will.

Scorpios are passionate and motivated. They are also stubborn and determined to succeed and they never give up, which is why they usually get the job done – no matter how long it might take. Scorpios work as hard as they do so they can eventually sit back and bask in the satisfaction of a job well done. As a water sign, they are as emotional as other water signs, it's just that they're not as likely to show it. They keep their emotions under check, but don't let that deceive you. They make excellent leaders because they are very dedicated to what they do. Hating dishonesty, they can easily become jealous and suspicious, so they need to learn how to adapt more easily, but their bravery means they have lots of friends.

Scorpios are unusually perceptive and sensual and are able to read people better than most. They are intuitive with a great understanding of human psychology. For their part, they live on an emotional rollercoaster. Some days they reach ecstatic highs and others deep lows. As a result, Scorpios can lose their temper and lash out when someone crosses them, so it's best to give them plenty of room, as you would an angry scorpion!

Extremely competitive, they love to test themselves in every part of their lives. Nothing really fazes a Scorpio who sees the world very much as black and white. Scorpios will use subtle manipulation to get what they want. They'd much rather take a scientific, even mystical path. There's an air of mystery about Scorpios and they can come across as being unusually fierce, probably because they understand very well the rules of the universe.

DOWNSIDE

Just like a scorpion, those born under the Scorpio sign can attack at the first sign of danger. Their sharp tongue is legendary and if they are backed into a corner their first instinct is to fight. They can be vengeful and spiteful when crossed. Coupled with their ability to be jealous, secretive, arrogant, and manipulative, it is clear that Scorpios can be downright nasty.

Fortunately, most Scorpios will never display the full range of their nastier side. They would rather keep these characteristics under wraps, which, ironically, helps Scorpio to be a kinder person. However, Scorpios can suffer from depression as they battle their own worst fears. But their determination means that they will pursue their demons with a vengeance and fight to renew themselves until they emerge from the depths regenerated.

LOVE

For Scorpios, love is never easy. That does not mean that it can't be rewarding. Casual flings don't do it for a Scorpio. With their black and white view of the world, they will either want you as a partner or they won't. For them, love means a deep, deep bond. Love has to be passionate, dramatic, and total. It can all be a bit too melodramatic for some people.

Scorpios can be moody for no apparent reason. They need their privacy and solitude. They are possessive and jealous, but if they're seriously committed to a relationship, they are protective, loyal, and faithful lovers through thick and thin. Scorpios are extremely dependable, and even more so if they receive the same from their partner. They are either in a relationship or out, and they are more likely to break up with a lover than to cheat on them.

Scorpios fully invest in a relationship, in their partner, in the experience of love, and the good and bad moments that are the inevitable part of any romance. A chart-dominant Scorpio can become obsessive. They will remember and replay every intimate moment you shared to memory. They might even turn it into a book or a song; many Scorpios are creative, working in poetry, literature, music, and arts. For them it's an opportunity to explore the depths and extremes of their emotionally intense behavior through a creative art form. For you, it might just be embarrassing.

Because Scorpios experience love so deeply, they can also feel betrayal just as deeply. Jealousy is a real problem for Scorpio. Every emotion

they feel – good and bad – is enhanced by their fixed and water-driven nature. Their jealousy can make them behave in unforgiveable ways because they lack the solidity of the earth signs, the rationality of the air signs, and the optimism of the fire signs. If they cut you off, it will be forever. Scorpios are ruled by their emotions and will react from the depths of their emotional extremes.

SCORPIO WOMAN

A relationship with a Scorpio woman can be a rollercoaster. With her obsessive ways and her deep emotions, she can be an incredible lover and partner. However, if you hurt her, then she will stop at nothing to get her revenge. She might try to hide her true feelings, but inside she will be a turmoil of extreme emotions.

SCORPIO MAN

When a Scorpio man is in love, nothing is too much trouble or too expensive for his chosen one. He will lavish his partner with time, affection, and money. Only the best will do for his loved one. Cautious, he won't reveal his true feelings until he knows they are reciprocated because he does not want to expose himself to hurt. And jealousy is never far away because he's a Scorpio! Just don't mention how great your ex-partner was to him or he will see red.

FAMILY AND FRIENDS

There's no shade of gray when it comes to friendship with a Scorpio. They are either a friend or an enemy. If a Scorpio does befriend you, then it's like having your very own bodyguard. They are the most loyal of all the signs. Scorpios are devoted family members who will do everything in their power to protect those closest to them.

Scorpios want friends who are authentic and honest, qualities they admire. The importance they place on humor and their love of a good joke mean that they look for people who share their witty sense of humor. Always one to push themselves, they will push their friends too, resulting in all kinds of experiences and anecdotes to share in later life. Having a Scorpio as a friend is never dull. They question and interrogate every aspect – not just of their lives – but also their friends' lives. You will find yourself thinking about things you had never thought about and doing things that you never thought you would do!

It takes a while for a Scorpio to open up, but once a bond is formed it will not be easily broken. They will go to great lengths to help their friends and to keep the friendship going. Because they are so sensitive, it is easier than with other Zodiac signs to fall foul of their friendship. Any breach of trust almost always means an end to a friendship, so beware of upsetting a Scorpio.

Scorpios are incredibly faithful and devoted to their families. Providing for their families and keeping everyone happy is what motivates them. They are very supportive and will do anything to help those closest to them. They willingly carry out their family obligations. They are happy to drive across town to collect aged Aunt Edna because that's what family members do. Scorpio will always protect their family. Creating a loving and comfortable home that provides a refuge from the outside world is critical to a Scorpio.

SCORPIO MOTHER

A Scorpio mom makes sure that the family knows she is in charge. With her family's wellbeing and comfort at the center of her world, she does everything in her power to protect and cherish her children. This can come across as being unnecessarily strict at times and to such a degree that her children can be just a tad scared of her. But they know that all that matters to her is that her kids are happy.

SCORPIO FATHER

A Scorpio father can turn his children into a bit of a project. He wants them to grow up independent but, at the same time, he wants to be their best friend. He will take the time to talk to them and make them feel special; sometimes he is better at talking to kids than to adults. He wants only the best for his children and will work hard to make sure that they get it. He knows how to make them feel special.

HEALTH AND WELLBEING

Prone to depression and introspection, Scorpio has to work hard to keep themselves on an even keel. But, just as they can be plunged into a dark place, they are very good at digging themselves out of that depression by indulging in life's little joys. Taking time to read a book or just sitting and contemplating as a scented candle burns is all it takes to lighten their mood.

Scorpios love exercise. The harder, the better. They have so much willpower and strength that they make great sportspeople. They never give up and push themselves as hard as possible. Scorpio men, in particular, love any kind of extreme sport. Boxing is a great sport for a Scorpio. Getting a sweat up is just part of it; it's a fabulous way of getting rid of any frustrations and irritations daily life throws at them.

Scorpio rules the sex organs. This is both a source of joy and stress. Sex is very important to Scorpio; it isn't just a physical workout, it is a spiritual union of the mind and body. When they're not feeling fully in tune with themselves or a relationship, then they lose interest in sex. The advantage of this is that Scorpio has learned that absolute honesty – in and out of the bedroom – is vital to help them be as healthy as possible. Scorpio will never lie or cheat, and their honesty gives them not just mental wellbeing but also makes them better friends and lovers.

MONEY AND CAREERS

Ready to work hard and passionate about what they do, Scorpios bring energy and ambition to everything. They set the bar high and work until they achieve their goals. They love to delve deeply into things making a research career, in any form, a perfect fit for a Scorpio. With their powers of intuition, Scorpios make great detectives and spies. Similarly, their psychological insights mean that they would work well in any field where an understanding of human nature is vital and, let's face it, today that is almost any profession from working in a start-up to being a politician.

Scorpio concentrates on the task at hand like no other sign. Committed, disciplined, and demanding, they have high expectations not just of themselves but also of those who work with and for them. They will always keep your secrets, so they work well in organizations where discretion is key. A loyal team member and a reliable boss, they protect those who work for them and have no time for their enemies. Do whatever is in your power if you have a Scorpio workmate or boss to not alienate them. You do not want them as an enemy.

Scorpios have a great knack for money, particularly other people's money, which they use to make more money. Always generous, they won't keep their money to themselves but are happy to share it out. Money isn't a great motivator, but they enjoy having it and being able to use it for good causes as well as helping those closer to home.

SAGITTARIUS
THE ARCHER

NOVEMBER 22–DECEMBER 21

SNAPSHOT

Element: Fire

Quality: Mutable

Keywords: Idealism, freedom

Planetary ruler: Jupiter

Rules: Hips, thighs, liver

The last of the fire signs, Sagittarius is ruled by logic. Inherently practical and with one eye on the future, Sagittarius seeks freedom and truth in everything they do. The archer is their symbol and it signifies their laser-like intensity at getting straight to the heart of the matter.

CHARACTER

A free spirit, who loves to debate the big questions in life, Sagittarius sees life as an ongoing quest to learn and experience as much as possible. They like nothing more than chewing the fat with friends as they ponder life's most philosophical questions. Being tied down holds no interest for them; they can't stand being bossed around and they can interpret other's opinions as nagging even when it is not. The obsessive need to learn as much as life can offer means that Sagittarians have many different, and seemingly contradictory, interests. The sign rules travel, philosophy, religion, and law, and brings with it a burning desire not just to see the world, but also to understand it as best they can.

Sagittarius is open-minded, casual, and easy to get along with, although really getting to know a Sagittarian is much trickier. Nothing really fazes them; their philosophy is that bad things might happen, but get over it and move on to the next thing. They believe that better things are always around the corner. Always logical, Sagittarians also possess an unnerving ability to see into the future, which is as much about their inherent intuition as it is about their clairvoyant abilities.

DOWNSIDE

Sagittarius can be a bit of a split personality. While part of them wants to learn and expand their mind and to push themselves to the limit, the other part of them is too impractical and disorganized to ever achieve their lofty ambitions. Terrible procrastinators, Sagittarians waste hours and hours as they become easily side-tracked from their original goal. This means they can be unreliable. Combine this with their irrepressible ability to overestimate and you can often be let down by a Sagittarian. They promise more than they can deliver.

More than other signs – they are linked to the centaur: half-horse half-man – Sagittarians love the outdoors, but, in another contradictory twist, they don't get to spend as much time outdoors as they would like. They love exercise, but are often very clumsy. Also, they can be stubborn and dogmatic, and they love to lecture anyone who will listen (and even those who don't want to listen). Coupled with their tactless nature, and an inability to lie even when it would be the best policy, Sagittarius can be a trying friend at times.

Since they have one eye on the future, often their impatience can get the better of them.

LOVE

Relationships pose a quandary for Sagittarius because they place such importance on their freedom. Commitment can be an issue for Sagittarius. Friendship is much easier for them because it does not compromise their freedom to such an extent as a romantic partnership.

Sagittarians can take a long time to commit to a relationship. Many never do and seem determined to become lifelong singletons, presenting a challenge in itself. If you do manage to snare a Sagittarian, then it will be the result of a lot of effort on your part.

But once a Sagittarius does commit, love is all about fun and having a good time. If they decide they want you as a partner, they will go all out to get you. With a boundless curiosity for everything life throws at them, they embrace adventure. Expect to be spoiled and be prepared to go with the flow.

Sagittarius lovers think big. They can be very intense and attentive, generously planning special things just to please their beloved. The privacy so cherished by other signs is not for them. They are open and tell you exactly how they see your future together panning out. When they are open, it means that they are sure you feel the same way they do. Until that moment, they will remain elusive and hard to read.

Sagittarians are often over-achievers and very ambitious, which is why they are attracted to successful people. As a fire sign, they value education and it is important that their partner is not only clever, but cultured. The intensity with which they approach everything means that at the start of a relationship, they will bombard you with affection. Whether that intensity can last will depend on how valued Sagittarius feels as the relationship progresses.

SAGITTARIUS WOMAN

Sagittarius women are outgoing, independent, fun women with a definite wild side. Sex is very important to them and they make sure they live life to the fullest. Friendly and kind, a Sagittarius woman is always exciting to be around. She takes interest in everything and is always up for new experiences. Because her freedom and independence are so important to her, she will always speak her mind. A great way of seducing a Sagittarian woman is to take her on an outdoor adventure for a first date. She loves being outdoors, doing any kind of pursuit. You need to match her love of travel and allow her to be a free spirit if you want the relationship to flourish.

She will not fall in love immediately. But when she does finally commit, she is loyal and devoted. She never settles for second best and would rather be alone than in a relationship that she feels is not working.

SAGITTARIUS MAN

Questioning everything and interested in everything, a Sagittarius man loves adventure and the possibilities that life throws at us. He wants to do and see as much as he possibly can, which means he can be restless and hard to pin down. If you share his love of adventure and a challenge, then you are halfway there. Once you are in a relationship with him, you will need to share his wanderlust to keep his attention.

FAMILY AND FRIENDS

In some respects, it is better to be a friend to a Sagittarius than a partner. There's not much that a Sagittarius won't do for a friend or family member. The only problem for a parent is that their Sagittarian child won't be around for long. With their love of travel and adventure, the open road beckons and they will willingly leave behind those closest to them.

Making friends is easy for Sagittarius; they love to talk and enjoy nothing more than deep and meaningful conversations with their friends. Humor plays an important part in those friendships and Sagittarians look for people who share their same clever sense of humor. Their optimistic outlook is attractive to others and, for their part, Sagittarians like people who won't tie them down. They value their independence too much to have to account for their every move. Dropping in and out of their friends' lives suits a Sagittarian best. With their sense of adventure and their willingness to try new things, they certainly make exciting friends.

Despite the high value they place on their independence, Sagittarians are incredibly loyal to the friends they keep. Months might pass without any contact but if you need help, they will do whatever is needed.

Home is wherever Sagittarians finds themselves. This can present a problem for family life as it means Sagittarians are more willing than other signs to work away from the family home, going abroad if need be. Sagittarius will do what Sagittarius needs to do and the family can fit around them. Their independence is sometimes hard to reconcile with the demands and compromises family life entails. Despite this, family is very important to them. Once they commit to a family, they try to make it work. They make a concerted effort to keep in touch with aunts and uncles and more distant branches of the family because they are, after all, family.

Sagittarius' famous lack of tact and direct speaking mean that honesty is prized within the family. They have a strong sense of right and wrong, which they pass on to their children.

SAGITTARIUS MOTHER

Once a Sagittarius woman decides to become a mother, she will protect her offspring and dedicate herself to making sure they have the best childhood possible. She prizes truth and independence and passes on those qualities to her children. She surrounds herself with all kinds of different people, so her children feel comfortable in any social setting. Fun is a key part of her makeup and guaranteed at home.

SAGITTARIUS FATHER

A Sagittarian father will always look on the bright side of life and brings up his children to always see the glass half-full. Prizing his independence above everything, once a Sagittarian man gets used to the idea of being a father, he will do everything to make sure his child learns to be independent. With a quick temper, a Sagittarian can sometimes lose his cool with his child but that doesn't mean he loves them any less.

HEALTH AND WELLBEING

Ruling the hips and thighs, Sagittarians are prone to back problems and issues with their sciatic nerve. Add to that their tendency to push themselves too far, then injury is often not too far away for a Sagittarian. They are the ones in the gym that have to lift the heaviest weights, do back-to-back workouts, and then wonder why they can't move the next day. It's always the Sagittarian who offers to sleep on the floor in the belief that they are made of sterner stuff than other weaker signs. They have not made the connection between their body's aches and the need to pay heed. Sagittarians need to learn that they have nothing to prove and that taking care of their bodies is not a sign of weakness.

Their determination to prove themselves invincible is at odds with their tendency to hypochondria. If any illness circulates, Sagittarius thinks they have it. For example, if they have a simple headache, a Saggittarian might think that it is a brain tumor.

Sagittarians love to eat. Food plays an important part in their lives, both cooking and eating. As they age, it is easy for them to put on weight. In

order to avoid putting on weight, exercise is vital. Overindulgence can become quite an issue unless it is tackled. It's fine to eat and drink what they like provided they keep a sense of proportion.

MONEY AND CAREERS

Sagittarius is linked to learning and higher education and many Sagittarians work in professions that require additional study. Since they love to learn new things, this is not a problem. Any career that requires learning works for them, from the law to teaching and publishing. Their love of travel means that any career connected with the travel industry would be a good fit. The only caveat for Sagittarians is that they do not like to take orders. They won't work well in any rigid structure, as their much-vaunted independence matters more to them than pleasing their boss.

Easily distracted and with a myriad of interests pulling them in different directions, it can be hard for Sagittarians to focus. They love the bigger picture and small details don't interest them. They find it hard to delegate because of their innate sense of equality. They feel they should be doing all the jobs themselves. But, once they are engaged on a project they will stick with it. 9 to 5 doesn't interest them. They will keep working until the job is done, even if there is the odd diversion *en route*.

When it comes to money, Sagittarius is the luckiest sign in the Zodiac. They make money and they spend money on what they like. For them, money is there to enjoy life. They want value for money, but they don't mind spending a lot if that is what something or some experience costs. Then they move on and make some more money.

CAPRICORN THE GOAT

DECEMBER 22–JANUARY 19

SNAPSHOT

Element: Earth

Quality: Cardinal

Keywords: Materialism, self-discipline

Planetary Ruler: Saturn

Rules: Knees, skin, bones

The last of the earth signs, Capricorn the Goat is the Zodiac's most organized sign. For them, it is all about following the rules and imposing order where they can. They are dependable, industrious and disciplined, with a love of structure and routine in every aspect of their lives.

CHARACTER

Capricorn's planetary ruler is stern and authoritative Saturn. In Greek mythology, Saturn is also known as Cronus, who is literally 'Father Time.' Capricorns are born serious. Even as children, they are like mini-adults with a maturity that seems way beyond their years. They come into their own as they age, and life seems to

improve for them because they take on board life's lessons.

Hard-working, Capricorns are ambitious and competitive. They are determined to succeed and will achieve whatever goals they set their minds to because they are in it for the long haul. Patient to the end, Capricorn deals with anything thrown in their way as they march inexorably towards their goal. Everyone can rely on a Capricorn because they take their responsibilities so seriously and because they are sensitive enough to pay attention to those around them and consider their needs.

Capricorns have a calm exterior; they remain cool and collected during a crisis even though they might be panicking inside, which makes them good leaders. That's because self-discipline is a virtue Capricorns prize highly. Unlike other signs – Sagittarius, for example – Capricorn knows how to be cool and collected in every situation. They analyze what needs to be done and then do it as efficiently as possible. They might appear a bit uptight and unable to enjoy the finer things in life, but that is not true. A Capricorn loves life's finer things.

DOWNSIDE

Capricorns are naturally cautious and conservative, which means that they can deny themselves new experiences because they can't predict the outcome. Their lives can become very predictable as they follow the same routine day-in-and-day-out unless they let themselves go a little. Capricorn is the least spontaneous of all the Zodiac signs and the most puritanical. Work comes first, which can be a good thing, but there is a time and place for everything. Lighten up a little and life becomes a lot more fun.

Relaxing is not a word that forms part of a Capricorn's lexicon. Work means money and sometimes Capricorn can be just a bit too status-conscious and money-obsessed. The more they work, the more money they make. Similarly, Capricorns can be too buttoned-up for their own good. They see talking about their feelings as a sign of weakness and avoid it. That's also because they don't really like to deal with emotional problems and would rather avoid talking about them than sorting them out. Capricorns need to understand that sometimes the boil has to be lanced.

LOVE

As with every aspect of their lives, Capricorns are deeply traditional and conservative in the way they approach love. The good qualities of Capricorn: their reliability, determination, and faithfulness make them a great choice as a partner once they have made the decision to commit fully to a relationship. Endlessly playing the field is not for them. They want a relationship that has legs!

Capricorns tend to take their time before committing. That's because they like to know exactly what they are getting into before they take on a partner. Capricorns will often be friends first with their lovers before they become romantically involved; that way they can avoid any unpleasant surprises. Slight control-freaks, Capricorns like to have some control of what's going on at all times. If they don't feel they can completely trust a potential partner, they won't begin a relationship until they feel they can. So, once a Capricorn does enter into a relationship, they trust their partner and are completely loyal.

The ideal sort of partner for a Capricorn is someone who is not only accomplished and smart, but who also shines in the world. Capricorn likes to bask in their reflected glory. Their traditional side manifests itself in their desire to protect those they love. They will defend them at whatever cost to themselves because once they commit, they want the stability that a long-term relationship brings, and they don't want that threatened. They are very giving and throw themselves into any relationship. Coupled with their protective side, this might come across as a bit possessive and claustrophobic if their partner values their freedom. But for those who want a reliable partner, Capricorn can make an ideal partner.

CAPRICORN WOMAN

She might appear to be as tough as old boots but, in fact, that's just a front. A Capricorn woman keeps up her guard until she feels that she can completely trust you. But, once you have proved yourself then she will let down her reserve and welcome you with open arms. She's not really interested in playing the field. She has a strong moral code and self-imposed boundaries, which she won't cross. Once she is in a relationship, she will do everything and anything to keep the relationship going. Her emotional depths might amaze you.

CAPRICORN MAN

A Capricorn man hates surprises, so he makes sure that he knows just what he is getting into. Dependable and devoted once he has his life partner, a Capricorn man loves the company of a vivacious partner because you take him out of himself a bit and lighten the load. Over time, life gets better for a Capricorn man because under a partner's influence, he learns to be a bit less regimented and more open and compassionate, making his life more joyful. Some Capricorn men fall into gender stereotypes and expect a traditional male/female split, despite the fact they are great believers in gender equality. It's just another sign of their traditional, conservative approach to life.

FAMILY AND FRIENDS

Duty looms large in Capricorn's approach to life, which sits well with family obligation and means that they are a reliable and dependable friend. You know that Capricorn will always do what they say.

Much like the paternalistic planet Saturn that rules Capricorn, Capricorn is the father sign of the Zodiac and, like Saturn, takes their responsibilities very seriously. That makes them popular with their friends who value their reliability. In keeping with Capricorn's conservative ways, they often make friends in the workplace because they have had the chance to observe the person before allowing them to enter the sacred space of friendship.

Capricorn makes a very good friend. They prefer to surround themselves with people who respect their privacy and observe the, admittedly invisible, boundaries they set. Famously private, Capricorns really don't like discussing their feelings with people and expect their friends to know this. While they may not collect too many friends in this lifetime, those they do admit will become life-long friends. Capricorns want friends who bring out the best in them. Don't expect a Capricorn to gush all over you, they will keep a stiff upper lip. Sometimes it might seem as though they treat their friends with the same efficiency as they treat their work. But, rest assured, if a crisis hits, Capricorn will be the first in line to offer help and it will be just the help you need. A friend indeed.

Family is everything to a dutiful Capricorn. Every aspect of family life matters to a Capricorn. They, better than many others, understand the importance of family traditions and rituals and they often carry on the same childhood rituals into their families – going on vacation to the same place they visited with their parents. Birthdays are important dates and they love to gather their family together whenever they can, especially at Christmas time.

CAPRICORN MOTHER

Saturn teaches Capricorn self-control and the sense of duty. The Capricorn mother's strength of mind and her ability to get on with family commitments without complaint comes from Saturn. She is invariably efficient and well organised and unflappable. Devoted to her loved ones, she will teach her children to be independent like her. She wants to work outside the home because it allows her to keep her economic independence. Often, she is not particularly demonstrative, but that doesn't mean she doesn't care very much for her family. Seeing her children with their grandparents fills her with happiness.

CAPRICORN FATHER

A Capricorn father can be quite an authoritarian figure. He puts his family's needs first and is happy to put in the hours at work to give them a good living. That means he can become a bit obsessive about his work because he is so determined to provide for the family. He saves money wherever and whenever he can, and, at the same time, he likes to economize. Good manners matter to him and he makes sure his children are well-behaved as befitting the children of a conservative Capricorn. He teaches his children to be careful with money and to be independent. He expects respect at all times and that his children do as he says. His children can rely on their father whenever they have a problem.

HEALTH AND WELLBEING

Ruling the skin and knees, Capricorns have problems with both. Believing that they have no limits when it comes to working out, they often end up with aches and pains and more serious damage to their knees and bones. A better awareness of their body's limits would help a Capricorn to stay healthier. Exercise is non-negotiable for Capricorns who work out better with other people especially in cardio classes.

The skin and Capricorns share a tricky relationship. Capricorns are natural worriers; they worry about anything and everything but, because they don't willingly share their emotions, they internalize. All that pent-up emotion has to go somewhere, and it's only escape route is through the skin. That's why they suffer from eczema and other flare-ups more than other signs. Capricorns need to reduce their internal stress levels and look out for other triggers such as certain foods that can cause skin eruptions.

Getting a Capricorn to slow down in a busy working day or to deviate from the weekend job list they have given themselves can be tricky. But, if they take time out to stop and have a coffee with a friend or a chat with a work colleague it is time well spent. Similarly, trying different types of exercise can pay dividends. Usually reluctant at first to try a spin class or a new yoga class, if they persevere, Capricorns will find the benefits far outweigh any negative first impressions.

A bath at the end of the day can be the perfect way for Capricorn to unwind.

MONEY AND CAREERS

Capricorns work hard, and they are good at making money. Of all the Zodiac signs, Capricorn would win the workaholic prize. Capricorn is the most ambitious and hardworking of all the signs. They will work in any organization and are happy to work as a team or to be the boss. Yes, they want to be recognized for their dedication and effort, but the best way of recognizing them is to pay them! Money is what it is all about. That makes Capricorn sound greedy and money-grabbing. While it is true that some Capricorns might occasionally over-obsess about money and the status it can confer, most Capricorns aren't like that. Money just allows them to take care of their family and perhaps to help the wider community. Many Capricorns have a strong social conscience and money allows them to fulfill their conscience.

As an employee, Capricorn will be reliable and trustworthy. They will do their job and then some; if anything, they might be just a tad too dour. As a boss, they won't appreciate too much fooling around in the office. There's little point ever challenging a Capricorn boss, they won't be impressed. Just keep your head down and get your job done, and you will win their admiration. They want their subordinates to take work as seriously as they do. Capricorns excel at any profession that needs precision and structure such as engineering or editing. They make great doctors and architects because they leave no detail unlearned – and they apply their knowledge thoroughly.

AQUARIUS THE WATER BEARER

JANUARY 20–FEBRUARY 18

SNAPSHOT

Element: Air

Quality: Fixed

Planetary ruler: Uranus

Keywords: Altruism, freedom, individuality

Rules: Ankles, shins, and circulation

The last of the air signs, Aquarius is the quirkiest of all the signs of the Zodiac. They seek to forge their own path through life and they are the last to join a tribe; they place too high a price on their freedom to do that.

CHARACTER

As an air sign, Aquarius uses their mind at every opportunity. The genius sign of the Zodiac, Aquarians are original, outside-the-box thinkers, who see the world in a unique way. For them, life is all about mental stimulation; without it they soon become bored and lack the motivation to achieve their best. Once they make up their minds about something, nothing can convince them to change their minds. Their stubbornness can, at times, be their undoing.

Aquarius has a contradictory, dual nature to their personality. They are both shy and outgoing. Party animals who crave peace and quiet. Driven by the energy other people bring, Aquarius needs solitude like they need oxygen to breathe. Without it, they will wither and die. Time spent alone allows them to recharge their batteries.

Uranus is the ruling planet of Aquarius and it gives Aquarians a visionary quality. They have an uncanny ability to look into the future and know exactly what they want to be doing five or ten years from now. They see the world as full of possibilities and are excited by what the future may hold.

Aquarians are the humanitarians of the Zodiac. Altruistic, they believe in the equality of all people and they see their role as one of helping people wherever they can. They like being part of a community. Their ability to look at both sides of an argument means that they are great problem solvers. These qualities combine to make Aquarius one of the more popular signs. People are invariably drawn to their quirky ways.

DOWNSIDE

Aquarians hate to feel constricted or limited in any way. Just as they believe in equality and freedom for all, they believe in their own freedom at all times. Their unconventional take on the world means that they can easily stray into eccentricity. Aquarians are always the first to rebel when there's no real reason, just because that's what they do.

Although they have a lot of friends and a well-earned reputation as a party animal, Aquarians can be surprisingly frosty. That is because they don't like intimacy until it has been earned. Their natural state is one of detachment. They need to learn to trust others and express their emotions in a healthy way. Their dislike of over-familiarity feeds into another surprising Aquarian trait – they are incredibly insecure. Riddled with self-doubt, largely because they question everything endlessly, their insecurity can actually hamper them on a day-to-day basis. If only they could relax and enjoy everything they achieve in life, then things would be a lot easier for the maverick Aquarian.

LOVE

It might take an Aquarian some time to commit to a relationship but when they do, you can be sure that it will last. The reason for their slowness is that they have to be sure that you are their intellectual equal and that you will allow them the freedom they cherish once they are part of a couple. Aquarius's individuality becomes clear when they are in love. Not for them the conventions that bind so many couples. Why would you bother to keep Saturday night as a date night? These age-old conventions strike Aquarius as odd but that does not mean that they love their partner any the less. The trouble is that sometimes the signals they send out suggest the opposite. If only Aquarius would realize that sometimes you just have to play the game. Your partner needs to know they are loved, and it isn't that hard to show them.

Aquarius's love for conversations means that the way to romance is to engage them in a good old chat. They thrive on intellectual debate, although you might struggle to keep up with them as they flit from subject to subject. Their seemingly random choice of subjects is not a sign of a lack of sincerity or insecurity, rather it is a mark of their curiosity. There is so much they think about and want to share with a potential partner. The upside of this is that they are never anything less than fascinating company.

Once they are in a relationship, Aquarius will do everything in their power to keep their partner happy. They are very thoughtful. They remember little details that make you feel special, like buying that wine you raved about months ago. Generous to a fault, they make passionate lovers once they are sure the relationship is going places. This stands both partners in good stead because Aquarius can be a bit melodramatic and they are known to break up just to make up on a regular basis. However, for the most part, they are loyal, committed and not at all jealous, making for a great partner.

AQUARIUS WOMAN

She is a bit of a contradiction. Even when you think you know her well, an Aquarius woman can surprise you. You get used to her slightly wacky ways and then she does something deeply conventional; she stubbornly refuses to do something for months on end, only to then suddenly change her mind. Life is never boring with an Aquarius woman. Just make sure you listen to her and make her feel valued at all times.

AQUARIUS MAN

Just like his counterpart, an Aquarius man is a mass of contradictions. He, too, wants a companion but wants his freedom. He wouldn't think twice about going off on vacation on his own and leaving his family behind. He attracts unusual people and unusual places. Rationality scores highly on his list of attractive qualities in a partner. Sometimes, he can come across as emotionally distant but that doesn't mean he doesn't love you, it's just the way Aquarians are.

FAMILY AND FRIENDS

Aquarius is invariably surrounded by lots of friends and has a packed social calendar. Their fairness and friendly nature attract people from every walk of life. One of Aquarius's great skills is their ability to be friends with just about anyone from that internet genius to the little old lady who lives on her own. They extend their friendship widely. Don't let that deceive you; you can be friends with an Aquarius, but few people will be admitted into their inner sanctum. That's because an Aquarius never wears their heart on their sleeve. They will only become intimate with a few people because otherwise they leave themselves exposed and vulnerable. However, once you are admitted into their close friendship group, it will last a lifetime. Also, Aquarius has very high standards of what they expect from their friends and what they are prepared

to give to their friends. They seek out people who are not dissimilar to themselves: creative, intellectual, and not afraid to tell the truth, however sticky that might be. Once you get to know an Aquarius at that deeper level, you will have a friend who is always prepared to drop everything to help you. In that respect, you become more like family.

Family presents a different challenge for Aquarius. They can choose their friends, but they can't choose their family. Dutiful and attentive of their family members, they will not forge close ties with relations for the sake of it, but they will do everything required of them. So, they will remember their partner's family's birthdays and make sure they are celebrated. They will turn up for all the celebratory lunches and dinners and do their bit although, if they were honest, it wouldn't be their first choice of how to spend their time. That's not because they don't love their family; they do. It is just that they find too much family time claustrophobic. However, if ever a family member is in need, Aquarius should be their first port of call. They will always do anything they can to help out.

AQUARIUS MOTHER

An Aquarius mother is no different from an Aquarius woman. She takes her highly independent and unconventional personality into motherhood. She sets her own guidelines for raising her kids, but then frets when they are at odds with her friends. She is always loving and devoted to her children and will put their needs first. Interestingly, given her kind and caring personality, she doesn't shower them with affection as other signs do. Her concern for the less fortunate in life rubs off on her children, who grow up to be as compassionate as she is.

AQUARIUS FATHER

An Aquarius dad can be a contradiction. While he adores his children and wants to bring them up to make their way in life with as much ease as possible, he might be off on his next adventure – leaving his wife to take care of them. Honest to a fault, he wants his children to be able to talk to him about anything. While he rebels his way through life, the thought that his children might do the same fills him with equal measures of horror and a sneaking admiration.

HEALTH AND WELLBEING

As we know, Aquarians tend to live in their head, so they need to remember to get off their butts and exercise as an antidote to all those hours spent hunched over the computer. They enjoy exercise when they can remember to do it, and because they are always ahead of the curve, Aquarians will have tried the latest exercise craze long before the rest of us. Any kind of class works best for Aquarius because they love being around people. They need other people to motivate them and push them to work their hardest. Solitary workouts and runs are not for them. A variety of exercise will keep an Aquarius interested and motivated. Aquarians can suffer from circulation problems and weak ankles, so they need to tailor their exercise accordingly. If they are going to dance, then they should seriously consider strapping up their ankles before taking to the dance floor. Walking is always a great exercise for Aquarians because it is low impact and low cost.

Similarly, with food, Aquarians can get so absorbed in their work that they forget to eat, shop, and plan meals. Food isn't at the top of their priority list and so they end up snacking on stuff that they should probably avoid. They need to organize themselves to avoid that pitfall. Just as with their exercise program, Aquarians love to be up-to-date with the latest nutrition and health advice, and that helps them stay healthy.

MONEY AND CAREERS

Aquarius is always looking to the future and careers that feature innovation suit them best. Cutting-edge and avant-garde careers entice Aquarians be it film making, technology, science, research, environmentalism, academia, or careers that still have to be invented. Anything that allows them the creativity they love and which they can immerse themselves in completely and push themselves to new frontiers. Aquarians never clock-watch; they will work all the hours needed so long as they are fully engaged in what they are doing. Any job that is routine and uninspiring will send Aquarius running, as will boring coworkers. They will always seek out the quirky in any situation because they crave that unpredictability and uncertainty that comes with anything new and unknown.

Aquarians are demanding because they set such high standards for themselves, and they expect those they work with to live up to the same standards. They love to work in a team because they are, at heart, social beings, but they also prize independent thinking and working. Don't expect them to spoon feed their juniors, but they will give them space and encouragement to reach their full potential.

Money is not a key motivator for Aquarians; it's a by-product of work and it allows them to be generous not just with their family and friends but also with the wider community. Aquarians have a strong charitable streak and use their money to help others where they can. For them, money buys freedom and that's what they care about most.

PISCES THE FISH

FEBRUARY 19–MARCH 20

SNAPSHOT

Element: Water

Quality: Mutable

Keywords: Compassion, mysticism

Planetary Ruler: Neptune

Rules: Feet and toes, lymphatic system

The last sign of the Zodiac and the third water sign, Pisces is the most emotional of all of them. Deeply spiritual, Pisces is represented by two fishes swimming in opposite directions, which symbolizes Pisces' inherent ambivalence: do they go with or against the flow? With Neptune as its ruler, Pisces constantly strives to reconcile their dreamy sensibility with our harsh world.

CHARACTER

A dreamer, sensitive, imaginative, and highly susceptible to everything in life, Pisces can seem like a porous sponge. They absorb everything life throws at them with seemingly no effective filtering system. They place a great deal of importance on the unseen, whether it's intuition or

emotions. That means they are under a constant barrage of information and impressions, which they take to heart, giving the result that many Pisceans are often generous to a fault, compassionate, and spookily psychic.

Pisces are selfless and will do anything to help others, sometimes to the detriment of themselves and largely because they are so empathic and emotionally sophisticated. That means they attract all kinds of people. With Neptune as their ruling planet, Pisceans are more intuitive than other signs and often have artistic tendencies that, coupled with their vivid imagination, can lead to great bursts of creativity.

Their intuition means that Pisces are wise and know not to judge others. They understand life's ebbs and flows better than most and they can share emotional intimacy with others, which few can match. Their tolerance and readiness to forgive is very attractive. They might come across as being quiet, but they possess a very defined sense of right and wrong. Their moral compass coupled with their gut instinct guides them well. When a Pisces speaks up, people listen. While Pisceans have strong convictions about how they should live, they have a 'live and let live' approach when it comes to others because they are so accepting and non-judgmental of others.

Pisces spends a lot of time day-dreaming, which allows them to escape from the harsher realities of life. Their inner life is a place of perfect harmony to which they retreat whenever things get tough, but at the same time, they love having a good time.

DOWNSIDE

All the characteristics that make Pisces who they are can also cause them no end of trouble. Pisceans are very gullible because they see no reason not to believe anything they are told; they are irrational and very easy to upset. That makes them prickly and over-sensitive, which can be hard to deal with on a daily basis. However, the biggest problem Pisceans face is that they live in a parallel universe where their grip on reality is weak at best. This leads them to being procrastinators who brood and then fail to act. Pisceans are hopeless at dealing with situations they don't like; rather than facing it head on, they do the opposite and wait for others to act. When things don't go their way, they are overcome with depression and lethargy. In the worst-case scenarios, Pisceans prop up their lives with excessive alcohol and drugs. They can be the own worst enemy, which is ironic as they have the best capability of any Zodiac sign to change their lives.

LOVE

Pisceans are total romantics and the most emotional and emotionally sophisticated of all twelve sun signs. They want romance and they want a soulmate. Pisces are passionate lovers who are in it for the long-term. They are not particularly keen on short-term relationships and flings. Once they commit, they will be devoted, loyal, and unconditionally generous to their partners, which makes the partners feel especially cherished.

Pisces' extremely developed sense of intuition can make them seem psychic. They can read body language better than most and know instinctively what their partner is feeling perhaps before they do. It is almost pointless to try to hide anything from them, as they will soon know something is up and that can damage the delicate trust between a couple particularly when a relationship is fairly new. If you treat them delicately, you will reap the benefits. Pisces might appear a bit whimsical and shy, but that's really because they are protecting themselves. They know that once they offer their heart to their partner, it's gone. As a result, they can need a bit of prodding to get them to commit to a relationship.

Once they are in a relationship, Pisceans throw themselves in completely. They love deeply and fiercely and will take it very badly if the relationship fails. They would rather work hard to make things work than rush off at the first sign of trouble, because they are often a bit too selfless. They tend to put their partner's needs above their own. This brings its own problems if the relationship is not balanced because they are vulnerable to being hurt and manipulated.

Because they are so dreamy, Pisces can be hopeless judges of lovers. They will look for that inner perfection in a future partner and will overlook all the evidence of their eyes. They will ignore advice and if they are smitten, any chance of rational behavior goes out of the window! Even when it's clear they have made a mistake, they soldier on bravely looking for the best in their partner and confirmation that their instinct was correct.

PISCES WOMAN

The mysterious Piscean woman has hidden depths and many seemingly contradictory layers to her. She hates anyone or anything that tries to restrict her because she knows how she wants her life to be. Carefully look at how she lives her life and you will see that she values her freedom above everything. Give her that and you can give her the companionship she craves. Her slightly standoffish manner is deceiving; she is warm, friendly, and regal in everything she does.

PISCES MAN

A Piscean man's quiet strength and self-containment make him an enigma. Romantic at heart although he might well deny it, he is a good listener. He loves to wine and dine his partner during long, cozy candlelit dinners, which make him irresistible. And if it does seem to take him ages to make up his mind, once he does so, it's for keeps.

FAMILY AND FRIENDS

Since Pisceans are so loyal and supportive, they make great friends. Sensitive Pisces is always the first to know when you are feeling down. In times of crisis, you can be sure that a Pisces will be there to lend a hand no matter what it costs in time and energy. Once Pisces has made you a friend, you have a friend for life; you can always count on them to stand by you, no matter what the problem is.

Pisces tend to be very demonstrative. They put a lot of thought into presents, which they know you will appreciate. But, they don't stop there. With their creative skills, they might write their loved one a song or poem just to express their feelings. They are open about their feelings and very much want their feelings to be reciprocated. The quality of any friendship with a Pisces will depend on you being as good a communicator as they are. Easy-going and selfless, Pisceans tend to have lots of friends from different walks of life because their unique powers of perception and understanding of people make them very attractive. Although being a leader isn't a natural characteristic of Pisces, their thoughtful, wise ways mean they are often called upon by friends and family for advice.

If Pisces sometimes seem a bit standoffish and evasive, it isn't personal. Pisceans have to have time for themselves and, because they find it hard to say no to anyone, they sometimes absent themselves just to avoid letting people down.

Family is very important to both Pisces men and women and they will go to great lengths to keep their families happy. They put their kids first and will do everything possible to help them achieve their dreams. Pisces always remembers everyone's birthdays and anniversaries, and it pays to remember theirs because it's the sort of detail that matters to them.

Home is very important to Pisceans and they have a great gift of being able to make a cozy home anywhere. Being a Pisces, they would love to live near water. Any water would do, but the presence of water is endlessly calming and reassuring to them. They can spoil their

children and sometimes find it hard to see any faults in them. That means their children – particularly Geminis – can run rings around their gullible parents.

PISCES MOTHER

Often quite bohemian, a Pisces mother likes all things alternative and is usually gentle and peaceful unless she's (rarely) pushed too far. Then she has a complete emotional meltdown. She is a devoted mom who will go to the ends of the earth for her kids. Perhaps her one weakness is that she finds it hard to imagine that her children could ever do anything wrong, and so avoids disciplining them.

PISCES FATHER

He wants his children to have the best childhood ever and will do whatever he can to make that happen. Creativity and imaginative freedom are important qualities a Pisces father wants his kids to nurture. Like a Pisces mother, he isn't the strictest parent because he wants his kids to be his friends.

HEALTH AND WELLBEING

Much of Pisces' life is led in their head, which means that headaches can be an ongoing problem for them. Coupled with their emotional intensity, migraines, and poor sleep can be another issue. Exercise and diet help but since a Pisces is so sensitive they can get easily disheartened if they choose the wrong type of exercise. They should avoid any exercise that pushes them to the point of pain. Pisces is best suited to more intuitive forms of exercise like yoga and Pilates; anything that simultaneously engages the mind, spirit, and body. It goes without saying Pisceans love any activities that involve water:

surfing, swimming, water polo, and water aerobics. The key for Pisces is to do with their body and mind what they do with the rest of their life; follow their intuition and pay attention to what their body is telling them. Only Pisces and not the local gym bunny knows what works best for them.

Pisceans enjoy the good life and are known to over-indulge. Too much eating and drinking and the late nights that go with that will play havoc with Pisces' health. They are easily wiped out and need to know when to stop. The odd party night is fine, but Pisceans need regular early nights and a good night's sleep if they want to stay well. The sign rules the feet and Pisces love a foot massage, in fact, any kind of body massage is a regular indulgence for Pisces if they can afford it.

MONEY AND CAREERS

Pisceans work best behind the scenes. If they can work with their creative skills, all the better. In an ideal world, they would work as an artist or a palm reader or yoga teacher – anything that is slightly offbeat. If it involves water as well then that's perfect, an oceanographer or a deep-sea diver, perhaps. Their kind and sympathetic nature is a natural fit with charity work. They are great problem solvers and will work hard making them great coworkers. Hyper-aware, they will have the office vibe sorted out long before anyone else, and there will be a queue of people wanting advice and reassurance. They will always support those who work for them, but if anyone is disloyal, Pisceans will discard them instantly. With a reputation as dreamy and unmaterialistic, it might come as a surprise to know that Pisceans are actually very good at making money. Their creativity means that they often make money as a by-product. For the most part, Pisceans don't give money too much thought. They are usually more focused on their dreams and goals, but they will try to make enough money to achieve those goals. Some of the richest people in the world are Pisces; the sign is second

only to Libra in the number of billionaires born under the sign of the two fishes. There can be two sides to Pisceans and money; on one hand, they will spend a lot of money without much thought, while on the other hand they can be quite stingy.

COMPATIBILITIES

Astrology isn't about judging. We've delved into each of the twelve signs, warts and all, and seen what makes each sign tick, what works for them and what doesn't. All the signs carry equal weight but, just as in life, it's a little more complicated than that. We all have preferences – that's life. And it is a fact of life that some signs get on better than other signs.

What follows is a breakdown of every possible Zodiac love combination. There are 78 in total, one for each pair of sun signs. While we concentrate on which signs make the best love matches, the analysis applies equally well to friendships. Where two signs are the polar opposites, they can use their differences to build a long-lasting friendship and, equally, where two signs don't click in love, they won't click in friendship.

To find your compatibility rating the lists are arranged as follows. Starting with Aries as the first sign of the Zodiac, there are twelve possible combinations (one for each Sun sign). It follows that the next sign, Taurus, will have eleven combinations and so on until the final sign, Pisces, which is left with just one combination with a fellow fish. So, if you are a Libra and want to know if you will get on with a Taurus, look under Taurus.

ARIES

Passionate and devoted when they are in love; Aries is also impatient and hates to feel trapped. Any lover or friend who tries to control Aries will soon be shown the door.

ARIES/ARIES

Aries is represented by the Ram, and an Aries-Aries combination can soon turn into two rams locking heads. That's because it's like looking at a mirror; instinctively they know their partner wants their freedom because that's what they want, but on whose terms? Fireworks are unavoidable. Two Aries will always be competing, but if they can learn to not compete with each other and put their egos to one side, it can be a great match.

Aries always wants things their way, but if they can work together and be a bit selfless, they can bring out the best in one another. Their strong personalities mean that the relationship can be hot and passionate. Naturally generous, two Aries will spoil one another. Because Aries tells it as it is, there will never be any problems with lying or hypocrisy. A word of warning though – both are prone to temper outbursts that result from jumping to conclusions.

ARIES/TAURUS

This relationship is all about getting the right balance. While Taurus represents love and Aries passion, the two go about relationships in completely opposite ways. Taurus wants to be wooed while Aries doesn't want to hang about. If both signs are prepared to learn from the other, the relationship can work because Taurus can help Aries rein in some of their madcap impulses and Aries can help Taurus to be less uptight.

Taurus is patient, gentle, and sensual, and Aries finds those qualities very attractive. Aries likes Taurus's stability and loyalty, and Taurus likes Aries' boldness. If Taurus can get Aries to slow down a bit and to appreciate just how sexy a slow approach can be, then the relationship might work. If, however, Aries finds Taurus too slow and dull and gets impatient – then the whole affair is doomed to failure.

ARIES/GEMINI

Both signs are high-spirited and easily bored, but this can be a fantastic combination because Aries and Gemini connect on both a physical and intellectual level. Aries and Gemini love any kind of activity and have a zillion different interests, so boredom is never an issue. Both value their independence and are excellent communicators. That's because, quite often, signs that are two apart in the Zodiac communicate and understand each other better than other combinations.

Gemini is a thinker who loves any intellectual debate, and Aries is a doer who tends to jump feet first into any new project, so when they pool their resources, great things can happen. Aries just has to be careful to not be too controlling, because Gemini hates to feel caged in. But because they approach things in a different-but-complementary way, it means these two signs are generally a match made in heaven.

ARIES/CANCER

This is a case of opposites attracting but it doesn't always end well. Where Aries is hot-tempered and dominating, sensitive Cancer is fearful. That means it doesn't take much for Cancer to feel overwhelmed by Aries. Cancer likes to take its time before committing, while Aries jumps straight in. This can seem very attractive, but both signs need to be wary. Cancer can be moody and Aries a bit too aggressive, and if neither sign listens to the other, then the relationship will suffer.

But, if they make the effort to listen to one another then it can work, because both signs are extremely protective of those they love. Cancer will give Aries the happy domestic life they crave, and Aries will give Cancer the devotion they love, which makes them feel wanted. If Aries slows down and pays close attention to Cancer's needs, then the two can really grow together.

ARIES/LEO

When two fire signs get together, it guarantees sparks will fly and a lot of warmth will be created. Passionate and dynamic, Aries and Leo can make a great match if they can overcome potential pitfalls. Both want to be top dog and that can cause friction. It's not just the big things they quarrel about; it's everything! If they can learn to take turns to be the boss, then harmony will reign, and the relationship will work. Both signs have a genuine admiration and respect for each other, and they need to remember that! While both of them are impatient and proud, they would do well to concentrate on each other's good qualities. Aries often looks to Leo as a guide and, surprisingly, can become quite docile when they are around Leo. Respect plays an important part in their relationship and with all their energy they can make a highly compatible and dynamic pair.

ARIES/VIRGO

At first sight it seems Aries and Virgo have little in common. Aries is brash and bossy while Virgo is quiet and shy. Aries' boundless energy is at odds with Virgo's slow, inhibited approach to life. It would seem that there is little each can learn from the other, but a relationship is possible if each partner is prepared to learn where the other is coming from.

Early on, neither sign might be able to see beyond the other's faults. Virgo hates Aries' aggressive ways and Aries is driven mad by Virgo's perceived passivity. But if they look beyond this then can learn a lot

from each other. Virgo can teach Aries patience and the importance of enjoying the moment, and Aries can teach Virgo to lighten up a bit. To make it work, both sides have to make a concerted effort to understand the other's approach. It might seem too much like hard work for some.

ARIES/LIBRA

As the saying goes, opposites attract. Aries and Libra lie 180 degrees apart from each other in the Zodiac. As a result, each sign possesses the qualities the other lacks because opposites attract. Aries is all about the individual while Libra is all about partnership. Aries is impulsive and the first to jump in and Libra is indecisive and likes to take their time before making up their mind. Libra is highly cultured, and Aries is brash. Both can learn and benefit from the other.

Another benefit of polarity is that the two have great sexual chemistry. When they get on well, it's a recipe for great romance. However, when they don't quite click the whole thing can become a disaster. That's because the energy of polarities can twist if the two signs fail to understand each other. If you take on board each other's differences, then this truly can have the makings of a great love affair.

ARIES/SCORPIO

This pairing is asking for trouble. When Aries and Scorpio get together, the sexual chemistry is off the scale. Both signs love power and when they work together they can do almost anything. The fly in the ointment is that while Aries is straightforward, Scorpio can be mired in jealousy. Sparks will fly as the two argue their way through their relationship. If Aries can accommodate Scorpio's possessiveness and tendency to lash out if they feel threatened, then the relationship might work. Both partners love to take risks and have adventures, the more the better. They will never bore each other. But this might not truly be a meeting of minds. Aries never hides their feelings while

Scorpio keeps things close to their chest, making true communication tricky at times. They can be like two soldiers on a battlefield either complete allies or sworn enemies.

ARIES/SAGITTARIUS

These two fires signs have a great deal in common. They both love new things and experiences and will try almost anything given the opportunity. You won't find them sitting around watching the world go by. They will egg each other on and can have a fabulous time provided they don't burn each other out. It can end badly because Aries is always in a rush and Sagittarius can see everything but the blindingly obvious, which can cause no end of trouble.

Even though they have so much in common – their energy levels, interests, and optimism – it can be hard for them to maintain a long-term relationship. They just don't have the stamina to see it through even though they enjoy each other's company. As a result, an Aries/Sagittarius friendship is often a better bet because they give each other the fun bits without all the exhausting bits!

ARIES/CAPRICORN

Over time, Aries and Capricorn will have to work really hard to make any relationship work. That's because Capricorns are never less than fully-fledged adults while Aries love to play the child. The two signs can end up irritating each other. Everything they do seems to be in opposition: Aries jumps in, Capricorn considers. Capricorn hates any kind of risk taking and Aries loves nothing more than a risk, so the two might be on a journey, but it's highly likely to be in opposite directions.

In a relationship, Aries will be impetuous and passionate and will pursue the object of their affection without really considering if they get on. Meanwhile, Capricorn will rationalize the relationship and work out exactly where it might be going (nowhere) so the chances of it getting

anywhere are slim at best. The thrill just won't last. Add to that the fact they are both stubborn and they might make better coworkers than lovers or even friends.

ARIES/AQUARIUS

These two are two signs apart and, as such, have a special connection. They can be great friends, but a love affair can be trickier. The combination of Aquarius' unique way of looking at the world and Aries' love of action means that they generate a lot of creative energy. Both are great communicators and enjoy new experiences and crave excitement. Spontaneity is the name of the game. Despite their mutual admiration, they can run into obstacles. They both prize their independence, but Aries can be too possessive for Aquarius who reacts by becoming standoffish.

Aquarius always has one eye on the future while Aries lives very much in the here and now. That means that the two don't quite make the match you would expect. Despite the special connection they share, unless they give each other time to really understand and reassure each other, any relationship will be short-lived.

ARIES/PISCES

Domineering, bossy Aries and flaky, fluid Pisces seem, at first glance, to be an unlikely match. If Aries is attracted to someone they will go all-out to get them but, when it comes to Pisces, their protective side comes out. The irony is that deep-thinking Pisces is the real protector. Their intuition means they can fulfill their partner's needs better than most. But, Pisces should beware. Aries can be too self-centered for sensitive Pisces who wants a little nurturing. Unless Pisces is prepared to do all the nurturing themselves, they can end up being a doormat, which Aries tramples all over. However, if Pisces is prepared to indulge Aries then they can be very good for each other. Pisces can better understand Aries than most other signs, and they can actively stop some of Aries' more excessive behavior. Whether Pisces wants to take the risk is another matter, and they might be better off looking elsewhere for their life partner.

TAURUS

Taurus is looking for emotional security and a partner who is as faithful as they are. Possessive, they aren't always as relaxed as they would like to be. Getting Taurus to be a bit more flexible will be a challenge for any sign.

TAURUS/TAURUS

A relationship of two Taureans can be a lifetime's love affair because they know exactly what to expect and what they are going to get. Taurus wants a sensual and stable relationship above everything, and if they get on, that's what they will get. The problems start when they disagree. Taureans are stubborn and opinionated, and two Taureans together can be lethal, particularly when you add their tendency to jealousy and possessiveness into the mix. They have to learn to disagree and still get on if they want the relationship to work. If they do, then together they can indulge in all the things that Taurus loves – romantic meals and cozy times together.

Taurus likes to take its time and relationships are no different. Neither will rush into it and once they commit, they expect and will give total devotion. Their dislike of change means that the relationship will last because neither will do anything to rock the boat.

TAURUS/GEMINI

This can be a tricky pairing because neighboring signs are always problematical. If they want their relationship to work, Taurus and Gemini must take their time to really understand its dynamics and then adjust their behavior accordingly. Gemini's symbol is the Twins and Taurus needs to know which twin it will get. Will it be the twin that loves change, and the freedom that comes with it, or the twin that wants the intimacy and security a relationship brings? Meanwhile, the bull Taurus just wants everything to stay the same. Brutally speaking, Taurus might be just a bit too dull for sparkly, intellectual Gemini. However, if they are both prepared to work hard then Taurus can help Gemini to get more involved in life, and Gemini can help Taurus to be a bit less staid. That said, Gemini's witty, sophisticated conversation might be a bit lost on Taurus who just wants a partner who likes bed as much as they do.

TAURUS/CANCER

What a great match! With Taurus's need for sensuousness and security and Cancer's capacity for nurturing and security, this is a combination that works. Partly because they are just two positions apart in the Zodiac, Taurus and Cancer share a lot of common traits. They both want a steady relationship above all else, and they both love to spoil their partner. A quiet night at home is perfect for both of them. They tend to agree on almost everything. They both enjoy nice things, great food, and all the comforts of home. Theirs is a perfect and harmonious match that others can only aim for. The only fly in the ointment is Taurus's pig-headedness. Sometimes, their determination to have things their way can send Cancer into a sulk. Taurus needs to be more sensitive and Cancer needs to be less moody and more willing to discuss their true feelings.

TAURUS/LEO

This can be a good coupling but only if each sign is prepared to accommodate the other just a bit. Dependable Taurus wants a normal life with its daily routine, while Leo loves a bit of action. If they compromise, it can work because they know how to pander to the

other's needs, as they are very similar. Taurus wants to be showered with love and affection while Leo loves to bask in adoration. Since their desires are so similar they can usually give the other just what they want.

Taurus and Leo both love nice possessions, a bit of luxury, and their creature comforts. Taurus loves to be wooed with all the trappings of romance, and since Leo is prone to extravagant displays of affection and gift giving, this can be a marriage made in heaven. A word of warning however, both signs can be stubborn, so each sign must be prepared to back down if the relationship is to last.

TAURUS/VIRGO

A great combination, the ever-practical Taurus and Virgo are drawn to one another because they both place such a high value on practicality. They both run their lives as efficiently as possible and appreciate the other's efficiency and common sense. They share many other qualities: hard work and a love of creature comforts, sincerity, and a great deal of integrity.

Virgo's cautious nature means it might take a while for the relationship to develop, but once it does, there is no stopping them. Taurus is more indulgent than Virgo, who remains slightly neurotic and determined to analyze all the options before making decisions. Once they do commit, in their search for perfection, they can be overly critical at times and Taurus can find that criticism hard to deal with and can dig their heels in, which infuriates Virgo even more. If the two can work that out, they complement each other well. Virgo is drawn to Taurus's strength and steadiness, while Taurus loves Virgo's quick mind.

TAURUS/LIBRA

This relationship can take a while to catch fire because, at first glance, there's little to connect Taurus and Libra. But if they persevere, this can be a joining of two halves to make a whole. Venus rules both signs, placing a high importance on romance. Wooing and being wooed is a key part of a relationship for both of them. They love luxury, any kind of culture, good food, and the security a relationship brings. The more time they spend together the more they can discover what they have in common. Libra knows how to deal with Taurus's stubbornness and can show Taurus that there is more than one way to skin a cat. For their part, Taurus can help Libra to overcome their indecisiveness and can indulge Libra, much to Libra's delight. But they need to take care; the presence of Venus means that both can be lazy and snobby with Libra looking down on Taurus and Taurus becoming more concerned with their possessions than their companion.

TAURUS/SCORPIO

Taurus and Scorpio are opposite signs of the Zodiac, which gives them a special connection. Any relationship is going to be spectacularly good or bad; it's either total love or total war. There's no happy medium with these two. Both are very passionate, so their sexual chemistry is a given, but since both are also very stubborn, this can prove a stumbling block if neither backs down. If they do, then they can make a great couple with their shared need for security and love of the good life. Both want continual reassurance; Scorpio wants to know that Taurus loves them and that's fine with Taurus because they want to know the same thing and they are happy to reassure. Taurus is always steady. For them, honesty and faithfulness are key while Scorpio loves to spice it up with a bit of mystery and melodrama thrown in. If Taurus can deal with that, then this relationship will work.

TAURUS/SAGITTARIUS

This relationship might work but, then again, it might not. It depends if both signs are willing to give enough to make it work. Sexually, they are a match made in heaven, but that's where it ends. Sagittarius thrives on constant movement and excitement, and guards their independence with a ferocity few can match. Taurus, on the other hand, loves their routine, their home, and just wants to be cuddled. To make it work, they need to give themselves time to learn and understand the other. If Taurus is prepared to wait it out, then Sagittarius will gradually come to appreciate the comforts a cozy home life has to offer. Whether they can reconcile their different approaches to life is another question. Sagittarius can try and spark steady old Taurus into action. If they succeed, it can make Taurus's life a lot more exciting but there's no guarantee Taurus will allow themselves to let go.

TAURUS/CAPRICORN

Together, Taurus and Capricorn have the makings of a fabulous match. Both are eminently sensible and practical; they share the same values and love sex. Neither likes to take risks and both are concerned with working hard so that they can afford the luxuries they both enjoy. Both set very high standards: Capricorn sets themselves goals they expect to achieve while Taurus has high expectations for every aspect of their lives. As a result, it's the mutual admiration club. The only problem is how to keep the spark going because they are just too practical and dependable. Add to that, that deep down they are actually more different than might be first thought and the two can hit the buffers. If Taurus can encourage the uptight Capricorn to relax a little and Capricorn can push Taurus out of their tendency to be lazy, then there's no reason why this relationship won't endure.

TAURUS/AQUARIUS

Taurus is known for being steady and set in their ways. Aquarius is known for living in their quirky heads. So, the question is, can these two move enough to make any relationship work? On paper it doesn't look good; Taurus the bull resists any mention of change while Aquarius is the most unconventional of all the signs. With few common interests, they don't really make the best love match. However, with a strong desire to succeed they might make better friends or business partners. Both love the sound of their own voices and have opinions on everything, so they are never far from an argument. Added to this, Taurus will wade in like a bull and Aquarius will pull away just as fast, the chemistry just isn't there. If they are being charitable, they can admire each other's qualities – Aquarius's dynamism and Taurus's reliability – but that isn't really the basis for a long-term relationship.

TAURUS/PISCES

Taurus and Pisces are two positions apart in the Zodiac. This gives them a shared empathy and a life lived to similar rhythms, which might come as a surprise because they are very different. While Taurus is practical, steady, and down-to-earth, Pisces is an idealistic dreamer. However, there is much they can share and much they can give to their relationship. Both value stability in a relationship and love to nurture. Taurus is able to help Pisces make their dreams become a reality. Pisces will offer Taurus all the love and affection they crave. Given the chance, a relationship between physical Taurus and metaphysical Pisces can flourish. Together, they can enjoy the kind of relationship which everyone dreams of. Never mind that Taurus can struggle to understand Pisces' seemingly superficial approach to life; that's because, in reality, Pisces is anything but superficial. They are the embodiment of the idea that still waters run deep. This match works.

GEMINI

Variety is the spice of life for the sign of the twins. They are attracted to witty people, they love to flirt, and will move on in an instant if a relationship fails. For them, life is about constant stimulation, but there's always the worry for Gemini that there's something better just around the corner. For Gemini, the grass is always greener.

GEMINI/GEMINI

This relationship will never be dull or quiet! Geminis love to talk, and two Geminis talk twice as much. Knowing just what makes each other tick means that neither will get bored as they bounce ideas off one another. Gemini prizes their freedom and ability to have fun and so, as a couple, they will undoubtedly be out living life to the fullest, and being the life and soul of any party. They must avoid the temptation to compete with one another; there's room in their relationship for both to flourish. The other fly in the ointment might be Gemini's inability to be serious for any length of time. With nobody to rein them in, neither party might give the relationship the sincerity it deserves. Sometimes, one of them will have to remind the other that love isn't just about fun and games. However, for most of the time it will be and these two will never suffer those meals eaten in silence, which other less compatible signs endure.

GEMINI/CANCER

King Edward VIII and Wallis Simpson were a Cancer/Gemini match and that wasn't a match made in heaven. Emotional Cancer is sensitive and a poor communicator, while Gemini has the gift of the gab. If they are lucky, Gemini can encourage Cancer to come out of its shell and Cancer can get frenetic Gemini to slow down so that they have a chance of making their relationship work. But, because these two signs see the world in such different ways, it doesn't look promising. They need to understand and appreciate that they are different beasts. Cancer cherishes everything to do with the home and Gemini could get used to Cancer's pampering if they allow them. But Cancer often doesn't know when to stop and can smother free-spirited Gemini, which sends them running in the opposite direction. Gemini is happy to act as Cancer's protector and will need to constantly reassure Cancer that they are loved. The question is whether they will want to do that.

GEMINI/LEO

Energy powers this relationship. Both signs are fun, outward looking, and optimistic. Gemini loves constant mental stimulation and Leo can provide that in spades. Leo will always try to take charge and Gemini likes to be free to make up their mind as they go along. The two might clash if Leo starts to boss free-spirited Gemini and arguments will be inevitable. Both love the limelight, which can be a problem as they compete with each other for center stage. However, a relationship between Gemini and Leo is about enjoyment and excitement. Although they approach life differently, they are well-matched. Gemini will over-analyze everything because they just love to debate while Leo jumps in without giving it much thought. If Gemini allows Leo in they might actually make up their minds for once. Another stumbling block could be their different approaches to fidelity. To Leo it is vitally important that their partner is faithful; for Gemini, fidelity doesn't really mean that much.

GEMINI/VIRGO

These two hit it off immediately and then talk themselves into a dead end. If the relationship is to flourish, they need to take time to really listen to the other one and understand how they view life. Gemini's approach is always split as befits the twins. They are invariably torn between two paths, but the relationship is helped by Virgo anchoring one half of Gemini so that its other half can flit around. If anything, Virgo can be too serious for Gemini. They need to remember to back off, particularly at the start of the relationship otherwise Gemini will run a mile.

Virgo is practical and demanding. They tend to criticize, which Gemini can bridle against. If they will just take a deep breath and allow each other to be themselves, they can learn a lot. Virgo can get Gemini to be more involved and to delve below the surface, while Gemini can inject a bit of fun into Virgo's life.

GEMINI/LIBRA

This is a wonderful match based on their intellectual compatibility and their mutual attraction. They will never stop talking, and although passion isn't top of the list for them, they are highly compatible. Libra represents balance and is a perfect counterpoint for the dual-natured Gemini. Both signs need intellectual freedom and they will give each other just that. They are great ones for coming up with schemes, which makes them great coworkers. Libra has the skills to make things happen and will push Gemini so that their ideas can come to fruition. Art and beauty inspire them both, although Gemini is more excited by ideas and philosophical concepts but the two are singing from the same hymn sheet. Communication is the key, but since Libra wants harmony at all times they will be reluctant to enter into the endless debates and arguments that fuel Gemini.

GEMINI/SCORPIO

This relationship is passionate and dynamic. If they come together, Gemini and Scorpio need to learn to accept their differences if their relationship is to succeed. If they can do this, then theirs is a formidable coupling. Gemini tends to be chatty, flirty, and intellectual, while Scorpio is more reserved, intense, and secretive. Gemini never takes their relationships too seriously because they see the fun in everything. This can grate with Scorpio who always seeks a deep, intense connection with any lover. Gemini's flirtatiousness can become a bone of contention because of Scorpio's tendency to be jealous and possessive. But despite their differences, this is never a dull affair. They will be happy to share life's adventures; Scorpio just needs to understand that Gemini will never fake their feelings, so they must back off. Gemini will commit when they are ready and when they do, it will be for keeps.

GEMINI/SAGITTARIUS

This match has all the hallmarks of a spectacular love affair. They are highly compatible and are great friends as well as lovers. They have a similar outlook on life and share a deep understanding based on an optimistic outlook. Sagittarius values their freedom and expects to keep their independence in a relationship. Gemini has no problem with that. Gemini shares a Sagittarian's love of adventure and new experiences. They love meeting new people and trying new things. Life for both of them is about getting to see and experience as much as is humanly possible. Sagittarius tends to be a bit outspoken and can be critical. Some signs would wither at this but not Gemini. They take it on the chin and move on because life is too short to hold a grudge. The reason this couple works so well is that they don't live in each other's pockets. They are truly on the same wavelength.

GEMINI/CAPRICORN

These two could not be more opposite if they tried. Easy-going Gemini doesn't take things too seriously while Capricorn takes everything, including themselves, super seriously. It might be hard for them to remember what attracted them in the first place. To make their relationship work, they are going to have to show each other a lot of respect. A relationship might be a step too far because they are so different. Capricorn follows the rules, while Gemini relies on their wits to cut corners and the question is whether these two can arrive at their destination at the same time. What's more, Capricorn is slow and steady, unassuming and quiet, while Gemini is the life and soul of the party, a ball of energy. In some situations, these two can complement each other. They are probably better suited to work together rather than to be lovers. Even a friendship can be a big ask.

GEMINI/AQUARIUS

Gemini and Aquarius thrive on their meeting of minds. Both are quick thinkers, full of energy and ideas and they have the potential to build a great relationship. Gemini loves ideas, whether it's thinking about them or putting them into action, and visionary Aquarius is full of them. Both signs value their independence and so would understand the other's need for it. They hate wasting time and approach life at full speed. They work so well on many levels that they can work to overcome minor issues, such as Aquarius's stubborn streak and Gemini's tendency to fuss. Both signs rely on their quick thinking and Aquarius can help Gemini to keep their focus, so between them they can achieve great things. They will never run out of things to say to one another because their minds are constantly whirring with thoughts they are desperate to share. The only problem with this pairing is that they are each a bit too independent.

GEMINI/PISCES

Very different creatures, Gemini and Pisces can, nevertheless, create a lasting bond if they allow themselves to be flexible. They are both empathetic and open-minded. Pisces uses their intuition to connect well with Gemini who, for their part, uses their quick wits and sense of humor to help dreamy Pisces keep focus. Gemini is all about seeing things from every perspective and Pisces is all about being open and receptive, which means the two function well as a couple. They also make great friends if the sexual attraction is missing. Sometimes, sensitive Pisces' feelings can be hurt by Gemini's tendency to speak first and think later. But, both of these signs are ready to forgive and forget and neither is likely to hold a grudge. That's because Pisces intuitively understands where Gemini is coming from and Gemini doesn't want to waste time being resentful. Their relationship thrives on their shared communication and adaptability.

CANCER

Loving Cancer wants nothing more than to find their life partner. When they do, they hang on to them for all they are worth. Cancer can be so keen to find that special one that they don't do their due diligence. Cancer is quite a catch; they are generous, devoted, and very caring, particularly to their family.

CANCER/CANCER

A Cancer/Cancer match ensures a loving and devoted partnership, which they hope will end up in happy families. Full of energy and drive, this pair are super-loyal to each other because they understand just how important it is to find their life partner. For them, a relationship is all about laying the foundations for a future together. They are caring and faithful and totally committed to one another. They want nothing more than the chance to create a family home where they can both shut out the rest of the world. They will defend their partner to the death because they know them better than anyone in the world, and they want the satisfaction that comes from sharing everything. The only fly in the ointment is that they tend to be a bit crabby (they are the sign of the crab after all) and full of self-pity. The trick is for each to know when a black mood is about to descend and then defuse it.

CANCER/LEO

This is a love match that can work if both signs are willing to adjust to the other's expectations. Domineering Leo wants adventure, luxury and passion, while docile Cancer wants to hunker down at home. If Leo can give up some of that luxury and Cancer can feed Leo's fragile ego, they might be able to meet each other's emotional needs. There are a surprising number of similarities; they are both extremely loyal and a tad possessive – even if for different reasons. Needy Cancer wants the security a relationship can bring, and Leo wants to be loved to bolster their self-confidence. Nevertheless, they can make each other happy because they both want a lovely home and a family and all the comfort and security that brings with it. Both signs are strong-minded, although Leo will always be the more dominant, and so they need to work hard to understand and accept each other.

CANCER/VIRGO

Over time, the bond between Cancer and Virgo will grow strong enough to turn into a loving, long-term partnership. That's because the two signs share similar qualities. They are disciplined and have a strong sense of purpose. Neither of them is interested in flings. They want a serious and sincere relationship on which to build a future. Hard work defines them, and they enjoy the trappings that it brings. This is a partnership built on admiration; Cancer appreciates Virgo's fierce intellect and flexibility and Virgo respects Cancer's dedication and inner resolve. Problems might appear if ever-critical Virgo hurts super-sensitive Cancer's feelings. Virgo deals in the here and now, and their practical solutions to all life's problems might clash with Cancer's more emotive approach. However, if Cancer can understand that Virgo isn't getting at them, then all will be well. Luckily for Cancer, Virgo's intelligence and sophistication means they will willingly subscribe to Cancer's approach.

CANCER/LIBRA

At first sight it might seem that a Cancer/ Libra match has little to recommend it beyond their desire for companionship and a shared appreciation of lovely things. However, that is to write them off. They actually share a lot of common ground. Both are looking for a settled relationship and the chance to build a home. If they can give each other time and really get to know one another, then they will grow to appreciate each other's qualities. Libra seeks balance and harmony in everything, and this provides a counterbalance to moody Cancer. At the same time, Cancer is able to help Libra overcome their notorious indecision. Both appreciate the other's ability to create a warm and welcoming home, which offers refuge from the world. Cancer needs to learn not to take everything so personally and overreact. Libra seeks stability and order just like they do, and therefore, they have the potential for great contentment.

CANCER/SCORPIO

When these two intense signs come together, sparks fly. That's because as well as strong sexual chemistry, they have much in common. Scorpio, ruled by Mars and Pluto, is full of smouldering, passionate intensity, which Cancer is drawn to like a moth to a light. Scorpio loves the adoration that Cancer heaps upon them. They have much in common and enough shared interests to keep the passion alive in their relationship. Making a nest is important to them and they will spend weekends buying objects to make their home as cozy as possible. Family motivates both signs and creates a strong bond. Communication is crucial to Cancer and Scorpio, but problems can arise if Scorpio finds it hard to deal with the continual changes in Cancer's feelings. Up one minute and down the next, moody Cancer can be a challenge for Scorpio whose feelings, while deep, are much more constant. Scorpio just has to learn to roll with it.

CANCER/SAGITTARIUS

This combination will struggle. While Cancer wants to love and possess and to settle down as quickly as possible, Sagittarius can think of nothing more than keeping their independence. That's not to say that they won't love each other passionately; they will. It's just that in order for the relationship to have a realistic prospect of survival, they both need to be patient. If they allow the relationship to mature, they will discover that they have a lot to offer one another. The question is whether they will get that far. Early on, Cancer will want far more of a commitment than Sagittarius is willing to give. But, as time passes, Sagittarius will learn to appreciate Cancer's emotional support. Whether Cancer can put up with Sagittarius's restlessness is more of an issue. Nobody values home-life as much as Cancer and unless they both accept that Sagittarius will come and go, the relationship will collapse. If Cancer can give Sagittarius free rein then it might just work.

CANCER/CAPRICORN

Facing each other from opposite sides of the Zodiac, Cancer and Capricorn have, like any pair of opposites, good and bad qualities. Moody Cancer has an emotional intensity and knows intuitively how things should be done, while pragmatic Capricorn is logical to the end and does everything by the book. But, they have much in common. Both signs are conservative and motivated by a desire to create a stable home life. Together, they can achieve much more than apart. Capricorn will always work hard, and Cancer not only appreciates their efforts, but can get them to relax and enjoy the fruits of their labor. Cancer will turn that hard work into a lovely environment for them to share. Capricorn will shield sensitive Cancer and will guide them to see the world beyond their own fragile ego. At the same time, Cancer will soften some of Capricorn's hard edges. Capricorn helps Cancer to feel protected and Cancer makes Capricorn feel loved, so no wonder this is a match that works.

CANCER/AQUARIUS

Do opposites attract? Sometimes they do, but for Cancer and Aquarius to be a love match they need to do a lot of work. Cancer is known for their emotional approach to life and their highly developed sensibility, while Aquarius is cool and collected. Cancer will retreat into their shell at the drop of a hat, while Aquarius is a party animal who loves to surround themselves with as many people as possible. They do share some traits: they can both be ambitious and determined. Neither likes conflict and they both like their own way (which can be its own source of conflict!). But, where Cancer values tradition and routine, Aquarius is all about spontaneity and the latest thing. That might briefly attract Cancer but, more than likely, they will tire of Aquarius' pursuit of excitement and Aquarius will tire of Cancer's staid ways.

CANCER/PISCES

This is a perfect match. It's a meeting of kindred spirits; both signs are equally sensitive, and they move to the same rhythm. Tolerant, sensitive, and sympathetic, both signs willingly learn from each other. Pisces loves Cancer's ideas, while Cancer is energized by Pisces' creativity and spirituality. Cancer is worldlier than Pisces, but that doesn't bother Pisces. Cancer might want a smart home with all the trappings and Pisces might be more than content with a simpler, more minimal existence, but such is the level of compatibility between them that this is not a deal breaker. They recognize that they have different aspirational goals, but they celebrate these differences. Theirs is a spiritual connection that brings to both parties the possibility of great love, warmth, and growth. The one caveat is that Cancer must be careful not to cramp Pisces' freedom in their desire to nurture and protect their beloved fish.

LEO
·····················

Leo is looking for love on their terms. They want a life partner and they want to call the shots. But because Leo is so charismatic and loving, prospective partners will forgive them for almost anything.

LEO/LEO

If the kings and queens of the jungle come together, it is one explosive relationship. The question will always be which one will be top dog, because Leo always wants to be in charge. This is a match that garners attention: Leo is outgoing, attractive, and attention seeking. The Leo/Leo combination is defined by its energy and drive. However, if they are to work as a couple, they need to tame some of their innate bossiness and passion. Both think life is about having a good time and they both want the best that life has to offer. So, they won't think twice about making sure they give their partners a good time. But their constant need for attention can become just a bit wearing after a while. The sex might be dynamic, but all those dramatics and 'look at me' antics will soon exhaust both of them. Leo is ruled by the Sun and that tells us everything. Leo always has to be at the center, so where does the other Leo go?

LEO/VIRGO

This is a tricky match. Leo is one for grand gestures, while Virgo obsesses on tiny details. On first meeting, they have little in common and will need to be patient if they want the relationship to evolve. That's if they can get beyond those first few dates because all they will see in one another is faults. Leo is outgoing, domineering, and charismatic,

while Virgo is withdrawn, passive, and much more versatile than the lion. As a result, Virgo might look on Leo as a bully and Leo might think Virgo is way too critical. If they can see beyond these faults, they might find common ground. Leo can teach Virgo to be less uptight and have fun, and Virgo can show Leo that patience is a virtue. Leo can also learn from Virgo to be more measured and balanced, while Virgo can lighten up a bit and stop being too judgmental. The question is whether this pairing has the necessary staying power to get that far.

LEO/LIBRA

Two signs apart from each other in the Zodiac, Leo and Libra's is a match that can work. They understand each other and what makes the other one tick despite being so different. Leo plays games; Libra flirts. But when Leo's energy mixes with Libra's innate sense of harmony, this is a relationship that has its own natural equilibrium. Where Leo is outgoing, Libra is reserved, and that works because they appreciate each other's qualities and see that they complement their own. Libra provides a good counterbalance to Leo's natural flamboyance. Leo doesn't possess Libra's charm, but that doesn't matter because Leo is spontaneous and will help Libra to make decisions quicker and then to act on them. Their relationship is characterized by warmth and passion because Leo is ruled by the Sun and Libra is ruled by Venus. This combination means that the couple will be able to nurture one another and form a lasting bond.

LEO/SCORPIO

A passionate and intense coupling, Leo and Scorpio are well-suited to one another. They share many qualities: both are fun-loving, entertaining, and intense. They are both extremely loyal and can be quite territorial about each other. Leo demands to be constantly praised and worshipped while Scorpio wants respect. But, each is able to give the other what they most want. Leo loves luxury and thinks nothing of pushing the boat out, which

Scorpio has no problem with. Scorpio's approval means that Leo radiates happiness and satisfaction. That's enough for Scorpio, who is happy to hide from the limelight while they pull the strings of the relationship from the wings. Leo and Scorpio understand each other so well that they form a formidable team that can face the world united. In spite of all this harmony, two such fiery signs inevitably clash, but they have the confidence to ride out these passionate disagreements and treat them as minor hiccups on the road to happiness.

LEO/SAGITTARIUS

When two such dynamic signs come together, they create a fiery and passionate couple. Both live life to the fullest and want it to be packed with fun and excitement. They push each other to try new experiences and aim as high as they can. They love to socialize; both are warm and charming and attract other people because of the good vibes they give off. They respect and admire each other and appreciate the other's qualities. Sagittarius can deal with Leo's over-exuberance, but there's never a dull moment. Leo wants to share everything with Sagittarius and do everything together. However, this can be a mistake because Sagittarius prizes their independence so highly and can easily feel they are being boxed in. If Leo remembers to let Sagittarius have free rein once in a while, then harmony will be restored in the relationship. All in all, they make a fantastic couple because they are so highly compatible.

LEO/CAPRICORN

A seemingly unlikely couple, Leo and Capricorn can, if they stick at it, become a force to be reckoned with. As they discover that they share many similarities, their bond will grow and intensify. Both of them love the good life; luxury and nice material objects matter to them. They work hard and love the rewards that hard work brings with it. Capricorn tends to be more conventional and conservative than flamboyant Leo,

but that doesn't matter to either of them. They understand that they can teach each other a lot and learn from each other in a mutually supportive environment. Leo loves a good time and can get Capricorn to let their hair down, while Capricorn can show Leo just how important hard work is because they never stop. They must not take each other for granted and make sure that they pay each other enough attention, in which case they will flourish. Having a lot of money doesn't harm them either!

LEO/AQUARIUS

There's never a dull moment when Leo and Aquarius get together. With Aquarius's foresight and Leo's creativity, they make a formidable pair. Both signs are idealistic and love anything new and exciting. They thrive on their mutual admiration. Leo loves Aquarius's unique take on the world and Aquarius finds Leo's charm and dignity attractive. Leo can help Aquarius see their ideas through to fruition because they have more determination to get things done. Both are independent and cherish their space. Conflict can arise if Aquarius feels pushed around and if Leo thinks that Aquarius is too off-hand. The best course is for each to respect the other's different approach. They need to keep all the channels of communication open to ensure the relationship flourishes. Aquarius will have to flatter Leo's needy ego and Leo will have to stop being such a control freak. But these are easily surmountable problems in such a sunny pairing.

LEO/PISCES

This can be a tricky relationship. The two signs are so different that it can be a case of opposites attracting, but it can also be a case of dreamy, other worldly Pisces the fish being gobbled up by Leo the lion. The positives are that each partner brings a new perspective to the other one. Leo is a natural leader and takes command of their surroundings, while Pisces is introspective and much more reserved. If they do care for each other, they can fill the missing parts in each other. However, the problem comes as the relationship matures. At the start, Pisces is entranced by Leo's bravery, but by the end they feel judged and criticised. Leo's initial attraction to the idealistic Pisces wears off as they become increasingly judgmental, leaving Pisces feeling bruised and hurt. If they can find a way through, Pisces will uncover a side of Leo that they show to very few people, and they will form a special bond.

VIRGO

Virgo's impossibly high standards make it hard for most people to make the cut. But for those who do, the rewards are high because Virgo rewards them with great devotion.

VIRGO/VIRGO

Two Virgos know exactly what they will get when they start a relationship. If they can deal with each other's perfectionism without going completely crazy, then theirs will be a great partnership. Practical and hardworking, they are devoted to each other, although you might never know it as Virgo hates public displays of affection. Since they operate on the same wavelength, there is never any misunderstanding or confusion about who is doing what. That makes them particularly successful parents as they are able to divide up their household jobs without any problems. Perfectionists, they share fabulous taste, so their home always looks perfect. They love talking and sharing things, and one of the strongest aspects of their relationship is their honesty and openness. They often don't need to speak out loud as they intuitively know what the other is thinking. The only fly in the ointment is their obsession with perfectionism, which means they can be overly critical. Fortunately, they don't hold a grudge and so tend to forgive and forget.

VIRGO/LIBRA

When these neighboring signs get together, it is like joining two dots. Both of them want a secure and stable relationship, and they work harmoniously together because they have the same goals. The more they get to know one another, the more they grow to respect each other.

They share many common cultural interests because they both love beauty and culture. A trip to the theatre or an art gallery is a great way for them to spend time together. Both are willing to see different sides of an argument and neither rushes to conclusions. Instead, analytical Virgo and thoughtful Libra will only come to a decision when all the facts have been weighed up. If this sounds dull, it isn't. The two complement each other; Libra appreciates Virgo's orderly ways and Virgo loves Libra's charm. Even when Libra doesn't quite live up to Virgo's idea of perfection, the two still get on.

VIRGO/SCORPIO

A Virgo/Scorpio match works very well. Since they are just two signs apart in the Zodiac, the two share many bonds. Both are loyal and their qualities mirror each other's. Virgo can deal with Scorpio's intensity and preoccupation with sex, while Scorpio can match Virgo's intellect. In fact, this couple finds each other so mutually stimulating that they don't need to hang out with others; they are enough company for each other. While Virgo can be quite introverted, Scorpio is much more outgoing, although they both enjoy being part of a community and helping others whenever they can. They both like goals and working towards them for the sense of achievement it brings. Virgo wants order in all things, while Scorpio wants to be in charge, and each allows the other to pursue their goals. If anything, their aspirations help to cement an already strong bond, which is built on passion, reason, loyalty, and energy.

VIRGO/SAGITTARIUS

Over time, this pairing might just find that their differences are too great to make it work, but it depends on how willing they are to try because there is much to recommend a Virgo/Sagittarius match. Both signs love to talk, particularly to one another, and bring their own unique approach to life to the partnership. Sagittarius is full of energy

and loves to be constantly on the move, while Virgo tends to be more focused and more practical. A perfectionist, Virgo's mission in life is to create and find perfection in all things, which the more casual Sagittarius might baulk at if it appears too early in their relationship. For their part, Sagittarius can bring a bit of excitement and variety to the pragmatic Virgo. While Sagittarius isn't much interested in the detail, Virgo loves detail. The trick is for them to concentrate on their respective qualities and to pool them to make a satisfying whole. Let Virgo concentrate on the detail while Sagittarius looks at the bigger picture.

VIRGO/CAPRICORN

These two signs understand each other so incredibly well because they both share the same element, earth. They are a perfect match and share so many values; each brings qualities that complement the other's. A force to be reckoned with, both Virgo and Capricorn are rational, practical, and methodical people. Virgo loves Capricorn's intensity and work ethic, while Capricorn appreciates Virgo's attention to detail and their intuition. Combined, they make a formidable couple. They both value material security and so will work hard to achieve their financial goals. Organized and reliable, they see life for what it is and react calmly to anything life throws at them. Capricorn can help Virgo to achieve their goals and Virgo can help Capricorn to be a bit less uptight. Together, they will have a happy life of domestic bliss, which suits them both to a tee. Lucky Virgo and Capricorn.

VIRGO/AQUARIUS

When Virgo and Aquarius come together, it can either be a match made in heaven or a bit of a disaster. Virgo is much more rigid and scientific in their thinking than Aquarius, who sees the poetry in everything. Some couples can thrive on their differences and grow together, while for other couples their different approach is a non-starter. Aquarius is inevitably more passionate and temperamental than logical Virgo, who pride themselves on their organizational skills and their sensible approach. Aquarius hates routine and likes unpredictability, which some Virgos will find exciting. For their part, Aquarius might be able to help uptight Virgo loosen up, although ever-sensitive Aquarius will have to learn to live with Virgo's criticism. Part of the problem is that as an earth sign, Virgo always looks to analyze and understand, while that doesn't really interest Aquarius, who is motivated by the spiritual and the mystical. If they can appreciate each other's different approach, they can learn a lot from each other.

VIRGO/PISCES

Opposites attract, and these two signs sit opposite one another in the Zodiac. Each brings to the relationship the qualities the other lacks. Virgo likes structure; they want order and schedules. Meanwhile, Pisces is instinctive and relies on their intuition to guide them. Surprisingly, this combination really works. They are easy in one another's company and bring out the best in each other. Virgo can help Pisces to fulfill their dreams and ambitions, while Pisces can give Virgo empathy and emotional depth, which Virgo seeks. Virgo loves their creature comforts and is mystified by Pisces' total lack of interest in materialism. This means they can have very different aspirations, but as long as they can accept this and support one another, the relationship will flourish. The stability that they find together allows them to devote time to helping others who are attracted to this dynamic and thoughtful couple.

LIBRA

Libra wants a mate. They love being in a relationship and they look to settle down as soon as they can. Known to be an outrageous flirt, it is all a means to an end so that they can find their life partner.

LIBRA/LIBRA

This can be a romantic and creative coupling because they know exactly what to expect, and they both crave harmony and beauty in every part of their lives. Together, two Libra balance the scales and bring order to everything they do. They love the idea of love and all the romance a relationship brings. They enjoy nothing better than spending hours talking over dinner or coffee, wandering around art galleries or seeing the latest film, just so long as they can do things together. Once they move in together, they fill their home with lovely objects. Neither likes conflict and they will back down to keep the peace. That means that two Libra will never push the other because they are so conflict-adverse. They know what the other likes and love spoiling each other. The downside is that they can spoil each other too much (watch that waistline) and their notorious indecision makes it hard for them to decide just what to do.

LIBRA/SCORPIO

These two want the same thing from love, making them highly compatible if they can last the course. Scorpio is all for the highs and lows of romance and wants nothing more than a mutually intense relationship with their partner. Libra is much more balanced (the scales) and wants everything on an even keel. If they can respect each other's differences and if Libra can help iron out Scorpio's propensity for drama, then these two are well-matched. Both will work hard to achieve the deep and meaningful relationship they both seek; Libra is never happier than when they are in a good relationship and Scorpio thrives on emotional and physical intimacy with their partner. Together, these two have the potential to achieve all kinds of things. They are both risk-takers and love a challenge. They need to pay attention to their communication because Scorpio tends to be secretive and intense, while Libra is much more open and relaxed, meaning they might misunderstand each other at times.

LIBRA/SAGITTARIUS

Two signs apart, Libra and Sagittarius share a deep connection and understanding, making for a great match. Sagittarius is on a continual journey searching for wisdom and adventure, and Libra can be their companion. Libra's love of beauty and art will only enhance Sagittarius's journeying. With an innate understanding of one another, the two signs feel as though they have known each other their whole lives but that doesn't mean they bore each other. Quite the opposite! They are great friends as well as lovers. Their interest and spontaneity keep the relationship exciting and new. They are both optimists who are happy to forgive and forget when they do argue. While problems will rarely surface, sometimes Sagittarius can be a bit brisk for sensitive Libra, and Libra can be a bit too strong for Sagittarius. But these moments are rare because Libra is the born diplomat who will go to great lengths to avoid conflict.

LIBRA/CAPRICORN

These two signs love being part of a couple and can make a good match if they find enough common ground initially. At first glance they couldn't be more different. Quiet Capricorn gets their head down and works hard, while Libra is a social butterfly who loves spending time with people and enjoying themselves. Libra is always looking for balance in life, while Capricorn is so busy working to earn the money for the lifestyle they want and the recognition they crave that a balance is hard to achieve. But, if they are committed, they can work together to give the relationship a shot. Both have different styles and approaches, which can complement each other, they just need to communicate so that they know what to expect from one another. Sometimes, this is easier said than done, as neither is particularly good at expressing their emotions. Capricorn must not put down Libra's natural optimism and Libra should try to help Capricorn achieve a better balance in life.

LIBRA/AQUARIUS

There's no end to the conversation with these two; they could talk all day and all night! Libra connects with Aquarius on a higher plane than the rest of us. Both love art and culture; they are very social, and both signs are concerned with the wellbeing of their fellow man. Aquarius is the most progressive thinker of all the Zodiac and combined with the harmonizing influence of Libra, the two can achieve great things. Neither wants to be tied down and they get along because they understand each other's needs at an intuitive level. The relationship will always renew because both are so enthusiastic and energetic. When Libra starts to be indecisive, Aquarius steps in to help them make their mind up. Libra can help Aquarius to deal with the disconnect between real life and life as they want it to be. Their commitment to one another and to the wider world means that they can help transform not just their lives, but their community's as well. Lucky them.

LIBRA/PISCES

There is much to recommend in a Libra/Pisces match. Often great friends as well as lovers, the two share much in common and are very compatible. They both love the aesthetic side of life, valuing truth and harmony above all things, and they complement each other well. If Pisces gets wrapped up in their fantasy world, more pragmatic Libra can bring them back to reality. They understand each other and should be able to avoid problems because Libra will go out of their way to avoid conflict, and Pisces is so empathetic they will sympathize with their partner. Both of them can be very indecisive and approach life in a scatter-gun way, which means they have a million and one projects on the go without focusing on any one thing. Since they both do this, it doesn't really bother them, but it is frustrating for others when they abandon a project midway. Libra must avoid making sensitive Pisces feel neglected if the relationship is to flourish.

SCORPIO

The sexiest of all the Zodiac signs, grand passion drives Scorpio. They want and expect to be transformed by love, which is a tall order for any prospective partner. But their charisma and sex appeal mean Scorpio is never short of admirers.

SCORPIO/SCORPIO

This is a match made in heaven or a match made in hell. Intense passion and unbelievable sex are just the start; both are obsessed with the other and, since they understand each other so well, the relationship moves at a giddy pace. That's great when things are going well but when two Scorpios fall out, its nuclear. The two can bring out the best in one another; they use their knowledge of the other's wants and desires to smooth their partner in love. Passion and determination will keep them together and if they are truly committed, nothing will tear them apart. However, if there's even a hint that one might not be truly committed, or they get involved in a power struggle, then the emotional fallout is truly horrific. If things do go wrong, they will always bounce back, but because they see things so intensely this is likely to make the pain of the loss of the relationship even more unbearable.

SCORPIO/SAGITTARIUS

This is a relationship that could burn out before it gets going if Scorpio and Sagittarius don't take things slowly. This would be a pity because it is a relationship that has lots to recommend it, partly because they are just so different. Sagittarius is all about independence and adventure while Scorpio wants to get as close as possible to their lover. Early on, Sagittarius might find all Scorpio's attention a bit too overwhelming and their lofty expectations of love impossible to attain. However, if Scorpio can be a bit less enthusiastic then the two can create an exciting and satisfying partnership. That's because they both see every day as an adventure that throws up endless possibilities to explore and learn. Travel will feature quite highly, and if Scorpio can be a bit more relaxed and Sagittarius a bit less impulsive, they will make a great team based on growth and mutual admiration.

SCORPIO/CAPRICORN

Cautious by nature, it might take a while for Scorpio and Capricorn to commit to a relationship but when they do, they have a chance to grow not just as a couple, but individually. Naturally slow starters, once they discover that they are not as different as they thought, they will learn that they can trust each other. As well as being a love match, they will be great friends. They will also learn a lot from one another. Capricorn will learn to have and show their feelings and Scorpio will enjoy Capricorn's protection. Capricorn should be careful not to seem too emotionally superficial and critical for passionate Scorpio. Scorpio wants intensity and security in everything and if Capricorn can remember that, the rewards will be great. From Scorpio, Capricorn will experience the pleasure that comes from knowing and trusting a person completely. Both will feel as they have found their other half and come home. What more could you ask for?

SCORPIO/AQUARIUS

If Scorpio and Aquarius do come together, it is the joining of two very different outlooks, two very different life philosophies, and two people with very different needs. This is a tricky match. Scorpio is immersed in their emotions and their inner life, while Aquarius is more cerebral

and much more interested in the external world. Aquarius is gregarious and outgoing; Scorpio more introverted and shyer. Scorpio gets enough gratification from spending time just with their partner; Aquarius needs a crowd. It's clear that these two have very little in common, apart from both being so strong willed that if they really want to make it work, they can. But it might be more trouble than it's worth. Both are opinionated and awkward when they want to be. They each expect to get their own way. Scorpio is obsessed with the how and why and Aquarius is very little interested in any detail. Aquarius is a free spirit and Scorpio is possessive. This is a volatile combination at best – and one that comes with a health warning.

SCORPIO/PISCES

These two have the makings of a great union because they share so much respect and understanding. Both are water signs and have a clear insight into each other's thinking and minds. Both are emotionally sophisticated, intuitive, and sensual. Scorpio tends to get carried away with their own secret plans and can withdraw, but idealist Pisces, who lives in their head, has no real issue with Scorpio's strange behavior. In fact, they can help each other. Scorpio will help Pisces realize their ambitions and dreams because they form a strong base from which Pisces can roam. For their part, Scorpio is attracted by Pisces' kindness and their gentle, empathetic nature. Pisces can defuse Scorpio's possessiveness and their rollercoaster of emotions. Scorpio is much more materialistic than the unworldly Pisces and they can have very different long-term aspirations. However, if they recognize this and work towards overcoming it, they will have a very happy and rewarding relationship.

SAGITTARIUS

Always looking for adventure, Sagittarius is a conundrum. They are excited by the prospect of a new relationship, but once it settles into a routine, they hate the domestic and want to head off for their next adventure.

SAGITTARIUS/SAGITTARIUS

Nobody knows a Sagittarius like another Sagittarius! These two are compatible when it comes to how they want to live. They both want adventures, they love to learn, are young at heart, and love nothing more than a full-scale philosophical debate. Both are easy-going and independent and have more than enough hobbies to keep them busy when they are not with their partner. Jealousy isn't really an issue for either partner. They are excited to show their partner what they have been up to so that they can share. So, what could possibly go wrong with a Sagittarius/Sagittarius pairing? Try the fact that they both tend to be a bit hot-headed and, since neither likes to be wrong, major arguments can erupt if neither backs down or they egg each other on with their impossible fantasies. When things do go wrong, they aren't very good at dealing with it, which can make things tricky. But, hopefully, things won't ever get that far.

SAGITTARIUS/CAPRICORN

Neighboring signs can either form a lasting pact or an ongoing war, and it's no different with Sagittarius and Capricorn. In many ways, they are opposites: Sagittarius is easy-going, and Capricorn is uptight; Sagittarius

wants to learn for learning's sake while Capricorn is goal-orientated. Sagittarius is outgoing, Capricorn is shy. Capricorn never leaps before they look, and Sagittarius always leaps then looks. Early on, it might be hard for them to see beyond the myriad of differences and each other's flaws. Capricorn can come across as being full of themselves and elitist, while Sagittarius comes across as unfocused and ill-disciplined. But, if they can look beyond each other's failings, they could actually build a long-lasting and significant relationship. By pooling their qualities, their relationship will become the greater sum of the two halves. Sagittarius can teach Capricorn to chill and be a bit more laid back, and Capricorn can teach Sagittarius to harness all their energy and to focus a bit more, thereby gaining more out of life. It could work.

SAGITTARIUS/AQUARIUS

Two signs apart in the Zodiac, these two will be great friends as well as romantic partners. Both are lively, uninhibited, and broad-minded. While domesticity doesn't much interest either of them, they can build a fabulous relationship because they are such great communicators. Sagittarius is attracted by Aquarius' unique take on the world and their creativity. Aquarius loves Sagittarius' initiative and their constant stream of new ideas. Both believe life is for the living and they will get the most out of it while supporting each other. It takes a lot for these two to fall out because they share so many ideals and they understand each other so well. Sometimes, Sagittarius is too selfish for Aquarius, who, in turn, is a bit too off-the-wall for Sagittarius. But these are minor gripes. All they need to remember is that communication is key. So long as they keep on talking and talking, everything will be just peachy.

SAGITTARIUS/PISCES

This isn't the most successful of partnerships, although they have certain traits in common. Both are seekers, and both are dreamers, but that's where the common ground stops. Sagittarius is more of a philosopher who is busy pursuing their many interests, while Pisces lives in their headspace. If they can overcome their differences, this can grow into a love match, although whether it will last the course is another matter. Pisces, as a water sign, can adapt to any surroundings, while Sagittarius is much more fixed in the way they approach life. Sagittarius has the versatility and gregariousness, which Pisces either lacks or isn't interested in. But, Pisces can be more tolerant of Sagittarius's off-handedness than other signs. Sagittarius's tendency to hot-headed outbursts can be too much for sensitive Pisces. Pisces's seeming passivity drives Sagittarius crazy. If both partners can see each other's traits and accept them, it might help them to become more self-aware and, in turn, in tune with each other – but that's a long shot.

CAPRICORN

Eminently sensible Capricorn isn't interested in flings and one-night stands, they are looking for commitment and nothing less. They want all the trappings that come with a traditional relationship.

CAPRICORN/CAPRICORN

These two come together to make a whole and since they share the same sign, they have the same goals and outlook on life. Capricorn is all about hard work, which means that these two will really know how to run their home and work lives. The challenge for them will be carving out time to just chill out and relax. Otherwise, they run the risk of leading a life full of work, obligations, and schedules. The goat, the symbol of Capricorn, is on an upward climb, and that's the Capricorn couple who are busy climbing the staircase of their ambition. They need to take a deep breath and look around them. Together, if they can avoid locking horns, theirs can be a mutually supportive and devoted relationship. Capricorns are loyal and charitable and good communicators. Their intense focus might put off other signs, but Capricorns don't mind as they are exactly the same. They have a great capacity for love, but don't need to swamp their partner. It's a great match.

CAPRICORN/AQUARIUS

Capricorn and Aquarius can bring the best out of each other despite being very different. Capricorn is cautious and rational and, above all else, a traditionalist. Compared with Aquarius who is an idealistic maverick, at first glance they seem complete opposites. But, if they

do hit it off, they can be an unbeatable match. There are several
issues that they need to work at. Both are incredibly opinionated
and unwilling to compromise, but any relationship will only work
if they learn the subtle art of compromise. Capricorn loves order
and routine, which Aquarius abhors. Aquarius's seemingly random
thinking can drive Capricorn crazy, so Capricorn needs to relax a bit.
Aquarius might find Capricorn's tendency to boss irritating, but they
can take comfort from Capricorn's willingness to give them boundless
support. Between their pooled qualities, Capricorn and Aquarius can
respectively learn to dream more and be a tad more organized, which
might be a bonus.

CAPRICORN/PISCES

On paper, this might not seem to be a match that works but, in fact,
the opposite is the case. Capricorn is regimented and puts work first,
while Pisces is more concerned with the world around them and its
emotions. But both admire each other and, over time, will build a
relationship, which grows stronger and stronger. That's because they are
both honest and can become devoted to one another if they do start a
relationship. Pisces will need to learn to deal with Capricorn's bossiness
and stubbornness and understand that's just the way Capricorn is made,
and it isn't meant personally. For their part, Capricorn is a homebody
who loves nothing more than hunkering down; Pisces has an innate
skill for turning a house into a home, which is Capricorn's idea of
bliss. Capricorn loves Pisces' empathy, while Pisces is captivated by
Capricorn's wit and their dedication to all things. This is a happy and
mutually supportive match.

AQUARIUS

Unconventional and bohemian, Aquarius loves their freedom. But when they find 'the one,' they willingly commit, although that doesn't mean they give up their independence or their eccentric ways.

AQUARIUS/AQUARIUS

Great friends but perhaps not such great lovers, but who cares? When two Aquarians get together, it's positively exhausting as everything is doubled. Twice the socializing, twice the commitment to making social change happen, and twice the amount of hard work. Theirs is a never-ending conversation as they discuss everything from the current political situation to what their neighbors are up to. Independent, these two spend little time at home because they are either working or socializing. They just love being around other people and jealousy isn't a word in their lexicon. Their mental connection is total, so it doesn't really matter how physically connected they are as that's not top of their concerns. Happy to spend time together doing whatever when they are not working, others can only look on with envy. The only problem they might encounter is that they can sometimes struggle to understand their feelings and the feelings of those around them, including their partner's.

AQUARIUS/PISCES

An Aquarius and Pisces partnership works just as well as friends or lovers. That's because Aquarius and Pisces share reserves of compassion and creativity and bring their shared idealism to the relationship.

Aquarius is always quick to come up with new ideas, which Pisces happily embraces. While both of them tend to be introspective, they are constantly looking for answers to problems and new ways of doing things. Problems can arise because Pisces is just too sensitive at times for Aquarius, who doesn't bother to hide their feelings when people aren't on the same page as them. Ever-compassionate Pisces can be a bit too self-sacrificing and gullible for go-getting Aquarius. They both need to be aware that just because they react differently to situations, that doesn't mean there's a problem. Happily, although they might disagree, these two tend to forgive and forget. Their intellectual and emotional resources will see them through the tricky times.

PISCES

The eternal romantic, Pisces wants to find their soul mate. The only problem is that despite their extraordinary intuition, they can be unbelievably gullible and too dependent, which makes things tricky.

PISCES/PISCES

Who knows a sensitive and emotional Pisces better than another sensitive and emotional Pisces? Same sign relationships can work either way; it's either a joyous union that plays to their strengths or a stressful union that highlights their weaknesses. On the plus side, both share a spiritual connection. They are great communicators and believe that their relationship is the best thing in the world and they will do anything to keep it. Keeping the peace is important and Pisces' tendency to passivity makes this easy! However, the downside to this is that together they can be a tad lazy and can bring out the worst in each other. Never ones to set any limits on themselves, they are life's great fantasists, which might or might not sustain the relationship. Escaping into their fantasy world and their unrealistic optimism is one way of avoiding conflict, but eventually the real world catches up with them. Although ever flexible, they will find their way out of that as well.

THE PLANETS

Our horoscope talks about what's happening in our Sun sign, but that's only part of the story. The other planets in our solar system – the Moon, Mercury, Venus, Mars, Jupiter, Saturn, Uranus, Neptune, and Pluto – all represent a different set of qualities and characteristics within us and in the world around us. Together, the planets and their interaction in our birth charts form the basis of our individual makeup.

Each planet has its own unique energy and each performs a different function in our horoscope according to which of the twelve signs it sits in. Our birth charts contain all the planets, but each chart is unique. The positioning of each planet will vary between different signs and houses, and they will all have a different relationship (aspect) with each other depending on their position.

In astrology, the planets are divided into three main groups according to their distance from the Sun. The personal planets are the Sun, Moon, Mercury, Venus, and Mars. They represent our personal drives and they make up our character. For astrologers, the Sun and the Moon (the luminaries) are considered planets, with the Sun ruling the day and the Moon ruling the night.

Jupiter and Saturn are the social planets; they represent the connections we make with our family and society at large. Jupiter is the expansive planet connecting us through travel, education, philosophy, and religion. Its opposite number is Saturn, which reminds us to follow rules and act within society's parameters. Uranus, Neptune, and Pluto, the furthest planets from the Sun, are the generational planets. Their slow orbits mean that their influence affects generations rather than individuals.

In addition to these, are the lesser known Chiron and Ceres, a comet and a dwarf planet, which don't fit into the above definitions but influence us nevertheless.

The inner planets each orbit the Sun at different rates, from Mercury which takes around 88 days to complete its orbit, to Pluto, the furthest planet from the Sun, which takes 248 years to complete a single orbit.

To learn where the planets were when you were born, you will need your exact time of birth and location. In themselves, planets don't cause anything to happen. Their significance is in their precise location and their interaction with other aspects of your chart. So, let's look at the planets in more detail.

THE SUN

SNAPSHOT

Rules: Leo

Day of the Week: Sunday

Metal: Gold

Colors: Gold, orange, yellow

The Sun is our life force; it is the essence of our being. Without it, there would be no life on Earth. We are reminded of the Sun each and every day as it rises in the East and sets in the West; it sets our seasons and marks our years. Not only is the Sun at the absolute center of our material world, but it is also at the center of astrology. The Sun is what we are. If the Sun is the central core of our being, then the other planets, as they orbit the Sun, each represent a basic drive within us.

A BIT OF BACKGROUND

Astronomically, the Sun is not a planet, but for the purposes of astrology it is. Astrology has divided the amount of time the Sun spends in each of the twelve Zodiac signs over a calendar year into roughly thirty days, (although scientifically this isn't strictly true, as there are at least thirteen and possibly as many as twenty-one signs). Your Zodiac sign depends on the Sun's position at the exact moment of birth, for example: a Taurus is someone who was born when the Sun was in Taurus between April 21 and May 21. Our Sun sign forms the basis from which everything else flows. However, a person born under Taurus with the Sun in their second house will be very different from a person with the Sun in the eighth house, for example. We will look at the significance of the Houses in the next chapter.

IN ASTROLOGY

The Sun is energy; it signifies power, position, and authority. That energy translates into life although the Sun is more connected with who we might become than where we have been (that's the Moon's job). It symbolizes our inner vitality, our guiding principle, and the purpose with which we live life. Its function is to guide us to come home to our true selves. The Sun is about being. In an orchestra, the Sun would be the conductor and the other planets and houses would be the players.

The Sun is our ego. It is our reason (as opposed to our intuition, which is the Moon); it is what we are. It sits at the center of our birth chart. To understand our birth sign better, we need to understand how our Sun sign works alongside the other planets and our houses.

The positive aspects of the Sun are our purposefulness, focus, creativity, and our pride. The more negative aspects of the Sun include a tendency to be judgemental, self-centered, willful, and even haughty. We connect to the Sun in areas such as play, risk-taking, creativity, generosity, and love. Innocent enjoyment without any particular ambition or goal helps us reconnect with our inner child. It's a way to live in the present rather than getting lost in the hopes we have for tomorrow or regrets from the past. The freedom to enjoy ourselves opens us up to the creative force of the Sun. It also makes it easier to give and receive love.

The fiery Sun is also about taking risks. It lets us express ourselves without worrying about the consequences. It allows us to transform

ourselves through our own bodies, minds, and spirits. By allowing ourselves to be open and to approach the world with play, art, imagination, and physical activity, the Sun shines brightly in our hearts.

The Sun represents courage: to act even when we are scared. Small acts of bravery train us to be strong when facing difficult circumstances. The heart is a muscle, which needs exercise. It can be strengthened by staying alert and being truthful when we'd prefer not to.

Self-confidence is another quality associated with the Sun and one that is often misunderstood. It is not about arrogance or power. A truly self-confident person shows compassion for others and is not afraid to reveal their own insecurities.

When we connect to the Sun, there is no need to be a bully or to grab the spotlight. Solar strength is patient and generous, it is creative and filled with the joy that comes from truly loving ourselves.

WHERE'S MY SUN?

Each person's sun is located in one of the Zodiac signs and that's the sign the Sun was in at the moment of birth.

THE MOON

SNAPSHOT

Rules: Cancer

Day of the Week: Monday

Metal: Silver

Colors: White, silver

Sitting in opposition to the Sun is the other so-called luminary, the Moon. Everything the Moon does is in opposition to the Sun. The Sun acts, the Moon reacts. The Sun is masculine, the Moon is feminine. The Sun represents our external self, the Moon our internal self. The Moon represents our deepest personal needs, our basic habits and reactions, and our unconscious. It is responsive, receptive, reflective, and spontaneous. In everything, the Moon is in opposition to the Sun: where the Sun is rational, the Moon is irrational.

A BIT OF BACKGROUND

While the Sun never varies, every month the Moon goes through its different phases. The Moon's symbol of a waxing crescent reminds us that the Moon reflects light from the powerful Sun. After the Sun, the Moon is the second most important planet, although to

astrologers the Sun and Moon are partners. The Moon is what animates us – just as it controls the ocean's tides, it controls the rhythmic ebb and flow of our lives.

IN ASTROLOGY

Just as the Moon reflects the Sun's light, the Moon in our chart shows how we can protect ourselves, as well as making ourselves feel secure, comfortable and safe. The Moon mediates between the inner world and the outer world of the Sun. Our spontaneity and feelings are ruled by the Moon. It's an important influence in early childhood, because the Moon reflects our instinctive reactions and responses. It tells us who we are by nature and instinct long before the Sun takes us down the path of self-discovery. That means that, for most of us, life will be an attempt to balance the solar and the lunar at all times. For the lucky few where the Sun and Moon occupy compatible signs in their birth chart, the solar will and lunar emotions will be in sync. That means they already have the balance between conscious and unconscious selves.

The Moon drives some signs more than the Sun, and this is particularly true with the Water Signs of Cancer, Scorpio, and Pisces. It is that hidden world, those secret dreams, the world that the inner soul perceives without revealing to the world that is a product of the Moon in our horoscope. So, for example, when we instinctively know what we ought to do but can't work out how to do it, that is our Moon knowing and our Sun refusing to go along with it.

The Moon is intuition, instinct, and gut feelings. They can express themselves in any creative field, in love and sometimes in business. Anything that we feel deeply about ourselves comes from our relationship with the Moon and the sign our Moon occupied at the moment of birth.

The Moon is our past and our feelings, while the Sun is the present and the movement to the future. The negative side of the Moon means we can be moody at times, irrational, and restless. The positive side of the Moon means we are creative, imaginative, sentimental, protective, introspective, adaptable, and intuitive.

WHERE'S MY MOON?

To discover the position of the Moon when you were born, you need to consult a chart. These are found online. Remember that the Moon moves into a new sign every two to three days. If your birthdate is one of the days when the Moon is on the move, make sure that you have the timings correct.

THE MOON'S NODES

The Moon is the only planet to have Nodes: a North and a South Node. In direct opposition to one another, they are not planets but points that take into consideration the position of the Sun, Moon, and Earth at the moment of birth.

The Nodes work on the principle that we are all born unbalanced. The South Node points out the parts of our character that may be overdeveloped and onto which we fall back when things are difficult. Conversely, the North Node highlights those aspects of our character that need more development. The aim of each of us is to balance our Nodes as best we can to achieve a better equilibrium.

MERCURY

SNAPSHOT

Governs: Gemini and Virgo

Rules: Third and Sixth Houses

Day of the Week: Wednesday

Metal: Mercury (Quicksilver)

Colors: Gray, yellow

Mercury is the closest of the five personal planets. These are the planets we can see in the night sky. Mercury is not only the smallest but also the closest planet to the Sun. It's never more than 28 degrees from the Sun and, as such, it has a special relationship with it.

A BIT OF BACKGROUND

In ancient mythology, Mercury was the messenger of the gods. The ancient Romans called him Mercury and the ancient Greeks, Hermes. Admired for his speed, Mercury was a trickster, musician, thief, and a master fibber; he could talk his way out of any situation. As the god of travel, one of his jobs was to escort dead souls into the underworld. He was also the god of boundaries and those abstract places that exist between here and there; between sleep and wakefulness and between life and death.

IN ASTROLOGY

Mercury's chief job is to determine how we learn and then how we express ourselves, not just emotionally but intellectually. Funnily enough, in today's world we often meet a person's Mercury through the written word, be it through email, Twitter, or texts, long before we meet the rest of them.

Mercury also represents our thought processes, and both our conscious and unconscious ideas. Mercury makes sense of things. Mercury makes us inquisitive, curious, communicative, and versatile. On the negative side, it can make us highly-strung, indecisive, and overly technical.

Mercury is restless. It craves constant movement; it stands for reason and the words we choose, and shows our thoughts, their speed and quality, as well as our brilliance or preoccupation with matters far from reason. On a physical level, Mercury represents our hands and our ability to use them, as well as the deeper connections between the physical universe and the divine.

As such, Mercury rules any profession that deals with writing, speaking, books, and publishing as well as any form of communication such as travel.

WHERE'S MY MERCURY?

To work out our Mercury sign we need a chart (available online or in books). Since Mercury orbits the Sun in just 88 days, in a year it will pass through all the signs of the Zodiac at least once and frequently twice. Consult the chart: a person born on March 5, 1996, for example, would have Mercury in Aquarius (their Sun sign is Pisces and their Moon sign is Virgo). Lucky them, because Mercury in Aquarius is exalted. This means that its drive and essential qualities are working harmoniously, with the result that they are inventive, progressive, and endlessly creative, with a particular interest in science.

MERCURY RETROGRADE

People who know nothing about astrology are often aware of the existence of Mercury retrograde and its negative connotations. We talk a lot about Mercury being in retrograde and the negative impact that can have on our daily lives. But what exactly is a Mercury retrograde?

Mercury takes just 88 days to orbit the Sun. A year on Mercury therefore is the equivalent to three months on Earth. During any Earth year, Mercury appears to travel backwards three or four times for at least three weeks at a time. This is actually an optical illusion caused by the fact that the Earth is also moving, but not as fast as Mercury (it is like being on a slow-moving train when a high-speed train passes by – for a moment you have the feeling your train is going backwards, when clearly it is not). Astrology believes that during a retrograde, information gets muddled and confusion is everywhere. Communications get messed up and travel plans can go wrong because Mercury rules both. Anything can go wrong from misplacing your mobile to forgetting your dental appointment to your plane being delayed or your laptop mysteriously malfunctioning. Irritating, annoying things that are not the end of the world, but which cause aggravation and stress.

The key to a Mercury retrograde is to remember that it happens a lot, and by knowing when Mercury is in retrograde, it's possible to avoid a lot of irritation by not scheduling anything significant, such as buying a house or signing a contract. Instead, use the time of a Mercury retrograde to revisit the past and to work on old projects. Never start anything new during a Mercury retrograde.

VENUS
· ·

♀

SNAPSHOT

Governs: Taurus and Libra

Rules: Second and Seventh Houses

Day of the Week: Friday

Metal: Copper

Colors: Green, pink

The brightest of all the planets, Venus is the second planet from the Sun, and the closest to Earth. It far outshines all the others and is more visible than Mercury, but follows the same pattern of appearing east of the Sun as the Morning Star and west of the Sun as the Evening Star. With a surface temperature of 900 degrees Fahrenheit (482 °C) it is one hot planet! Like the Moon, Venus is considered to be feminine.

A BIT OF BACKGROUND

To the ancient Romans, Venus (known to the ancient Greeks as Aphrodite) was the goddess of love, beauty, sex, and desire. The unfaithful wife of Vulcan, the lover of Adonis and her particular favorite, Mars, she was the long-time companion of Eros. The ancient Aztecs of Central America considered a Venus retrograde a particularly dangerous time.

IN ASTROLOGY

Astrologers have always associated Venus with love, beauty, and luxury. She also rules art, literature, and music. Venus is the planet that rules the forces of physical and emotional attraction. She determines our ability to attract compatible people and to form not just close personal relationships, but also business relationships.

Venus creates beauty and shows us where to look for it. Venus can even find beauty in hardship and experiences that most people would consider negative. For that reason, it has little to do with reason and common sense, especially when it is exalted and set in the sign of Pisces, which is also the sign of Mercury's fall.

Venus' main role is to balance our entire existence, but because Venus rules both Taurus and Libra – two signs that have difficulty accepting each other – conflict can follow and Venus hates conflict. Conflict is hidden in Venus, and therefore we need to constantly check to make sure the balance is maintained. Venus as the goddess of love and romance understands both physical love, and platonic love. Always a peacemaker, Venus brings the desire for harmony, proportion, and balance; she is the one to realize that morals and obligation have nothing to do with love, passion, or creation.

WHERE'S MY VENUS?

To discover where Venus was on our chosen birthday of March 5, 1996, we need a chart, which can be found online or in books. Venus entered Taurus on that day at 16.01 (GMT) so it depends what the time of birth was. Before 16.01, Venus was in Aquarius. Since Venus rules Taurus, those born after 16.01 are completely at home and enjoy all of life's pleasures, preferably with the same person. For those born earlier in the day, an Aquarius sign means they are more independent and less interested in those daily luxuries.

VENUS RETROGRADE

It takes Venus 255 days to orbit the Sun. Venus retrogrades every eighteen months for around six weeks each time. There was no retrograde in 2019, but 2020 saw a Venus retrograde from May 13 until June 25. Of all the planets, Venus spends the least amount of time in retrograde (although Mars' retrogrades are the least frequent of all planetary retrogrades) but as with the Mercury retrograde, when it does happen, the change is noticeable, and generally leads to a feeling of chaos. Astrologers think of a Venus retrograde as a time of uncertainty, misinterpretation, passivity, distraction, and unfulfilled desires, both in romance and in financial matters.

Because Venus rules love, relationships are affected. Not just romantic relationships, but also artistic and creative ones. Romantic relationships which are already under strain might struggle during a Venus retrograde. As with Mercury and Mars retrograde, sometimes old lovers reappear looking for healing and closure. When Venus is retrograde, it is not a good time to get married! Wait until Venus has moved on.

Similarly, because of Venus' role in our financial dealings, avoid making any large financial commitments during a retrograde. That mortgage, car deal, or expensive jewelry can wait a few weeks. On a more positive note, the tension we experience during a Venus retrograde can help us gain perspective.

MARS

SNAPSHOT

Governs: Aries and Scorpio

Rules: First and Eighth Houses

Day of the Week: Tuesday

Metal: Iron

Color: Red

The fourth planet from the Sun, the red planet Mars
is the closest planet to Earth. It takes Mars almost
two years – 687 days – to orbit the Sun. Its red glow
is actually caused by iron oxide in its rocky soil. In
astrology, Mars reflects some of the basic psychological
traits of our personality – it's the planet of energy.

A BIT OF BACKGROUND

Mars's fiery appearance led the ancient Romans to name their god of
war after the planet. In ancient Greece Ares, as he was known, had
a pretty tough time. The other Greek gods, apart from Aphrodite
(Venus) who was in love with him, constantly humiliated him. For
ancient astrologers, Mars was a dangerous planet associated with
violence, death, and destruction. As late as the fifteenth century,
astrologers were still linking the planet with any kind of evil. Today,

astrologers still connect Mars to war and destruction. In fact, Mars's energy can be constructive or destructive depending on how we channel it.

IN ASTROLOGY

Mars is the energy principle in our horoscope. It rules our actions, our initiative and our drive. The sign Mars was in when we were born determines how and where we will direct our energy. Mars is our unconscious nature and illustrates how the Sun (our ego) and the Moon (our desires) express themselves. If we try to restrict Mars, it leads to unhealthy inhibitions and a build-up of anger and frustration. If we are brave enough to live up to our full potential, Mars can provide us with the energy we need to follow our plans and reach our goals.

Astrology depicts Mars as a male force, which is fast, instinctive, rash, aggressive, pushy, and angry. But if we use its energy wisely, depending on which Zodiac sign Mars sits in, it helps us reach our goals. When Mars is weak, for example when it is in Cancer, its fall sign, it will bend the energy of a person and lead to destructive or self-destructive behavior. When it's in its exalted sign, Capricorn, energy and ambitions are well focused.

Mars represents our need for conflict, and to fight for what we deserve or want to take for ourselves. In itself, it has no awareness or common sense and needs the help of the Sun and Mercury. Neither can it understand emotion without the help of the Moon and Venus. Emotion is its biggest challenge and its greatest reward.

WHERE'S MY MARS?

Mars typically spends between six and eight weeks in each Zodiac sign although when it sits in retrograde it remains in a sign for much longer – around two and a half months. To find which sign Mars was in at the moment of our birth, we need to consult a chart either online or in a book. For the birthday of March 5, 1996, Mars was in Pisces, which it

entered on February 15 and stayed in until March 24. Mars in Pisces means that this person is generous, moody, restless, and very intuitive (a Piscean trait). When life gets too much for them, they switch off, their energy disappears, and they mope.

MARS RETROGRADE

Mars goes into retrograde every 22 months for around 11 weeks. In 2020, Mars retrograde started on September 9th and lasted until November 13th. Typically, when the fiery planet goes into retrograde its energy gets diverted. When it is not in retrograde, its energy can be positive, but once it's in retrograde, beware! All aggression and irritation tends to be pushed underground so everything takes longer. It is not a time to get into conflict because it will invariably end badly. Instead, the most productive approach to a Mars retrograde is to take a step back and use it as a time for introspection and reflection. Mars retrogrades always bring uncertainty and can undermine even the most positive of people. Avoid making any major decisions at this time; do your research and make plans then act once the retrograde has passed.

THE HOUSES

The three pillars of astrology are the Zodiac signs, the planets, and the houses. It's now time to look at the houses. They put the meat onto the bones and take astrology to a deeper level. An understanding of how the houses work is essential to understand our birth charts. Each planet, asteroid, or celestial point exists within a house, and that placement offers invaluable insight, not just about our personality, but also about how we live within the world. The houses are a roadmap to understand our past, present, and our future. The houses are what make astrology so special.

THE BASICS

The birth chart is divided into twelve equal sections, each one called a House. The houses are not the same as the signs on the Zodiac, which is based on the sun's yearly rotational movement. The houses reflect the Earth's 24-hour rotation around its axis. Astrologers fuse these two systems together when they read a birth chart.

Since the houses rotate every single 24 hours, it is absolutely imperative to use our exact time of birth when we calculate a chart. The houses also move every four minutes, so even people born on the same day in the same place will have very different natal charts depending on when they were born. The function of the houses is to show the gifts or obstacles we will face in our lifetime. So, if the birth time is incorrect, everything in the chart will be inaccurate.

When we trace our birth chart, it's not unusual to find there are many planets in certain houses (four or more planets in a single house is called a stellium), while others may be completely empty. That's absolutely normal. The birth chart is simply a snapshot of the sky at our moment of birth, and since most celestial bodies travel in clusters, they often stay close together. However, although the empty areas don't signify deficiencies, the locations of the planets do reveal important information as we shall see.

EMPTY HOUSES

There are ten planets and twelve houses, so there are bound to be empty houses somewhere in our charts. An empty house does not signify a lack. Instead, it often means that the usual concerns of that house are not an important consideration in our chart. It's a bit more complicated than that, but we will cover that later on.

For now, let's look at the houses.

THE FIRST HOUSE

The First House defines who we are: the body we are born with, our physical appearance, and our will. Defined by the Ascendant (see glossary), the First House sets your personality. The planets that occupy the First House tend to have a huge influence on how our lives unfurl.

This is the first stop in the cycle and the natal planets that move into this house set our goals, and determine how we will see the world and how we will behave in the world. The first house also determines the image that we will project onto the world, perhaps through things that seem superficial, such as the clothes we wear, the home we live in, or the car we drive.

If we have any planets in the first house, we will identify strongly with them. They make such an impression on our character that we can't help but be aware of them. Similarly, the planets will determine the relationship we have with our bodies and even our energy levels.

PLANETS IN THE FIRST HOUSE

Once we know which planets fall in the first house, we can work out how they influence us. Several planets in a house will emphasize its importance within the birth chart. Below is a list of the main attributes each planet brings.

THE SUN

Self-development and a strong sense of identity and leadership potentially all feature. Active and enterprising, with a sense of pride in personal achievements, the Sun's presence suggests the importance of the influence of father figures.

THE MOON

Mothers are very influential when the Moon is present in the first house. Emotions tend to sit on the surface and no-one is left in any doubt as to what those feelings are. Physical appearance matters a lot.

MERCURY

Curious, eager to learn and more than happy to share ideas and views with others, Mercury means communication. Talking, in particular, is key in making connections with others.

VENUS

Physical beauty and appearance are important and looking good matters. Being a peacemaker is also important, as is being sociable and friendly.

MARS

Taking the initiative to demonstrate strength and will is typical of Mars in this house; fighting for what they believe in and want is second nature. Passions and anger are clear for all to see.

JUPITER

The possibility for self-improvement and development attracts people, as does the optimistic and philosophical nature of those with Jupiter in their first house. They also tend to put on weight!

SATURN

Preparation is all, and a sense of responsibility and duty pervades everything Saturn's presence in the first house brings. Insecurity about what others think means that fear of being hurt determines every action.

URANUS

With an unusual demeanor, they possess a sense of alienation, so that feeling out of step with others is typical. An outlier, Uranus's presence brings fresh insight to different situations.

NEPTUNE

Impressionable and intuitive, and hard to categorize, glamorous Neptune brings an added dimension and an extra sense with which to navigate the world.

PLUTO

Private, with a magnetic personality and a need to control mark Pluto's presence. It is quite possible that Pluto's presence will bring about several distinct episodes across a lifetime.

ZODIAC SIGNS AND THE FIRST HOUSE

We can further refine our birth charts by looking at the signs the first house planets sit in, and also the signs on the cusp of the first house in the chart.

ARIES

Self-motivated and keen to get a move on, Aries always take the initiative – right from birth!

TAURUS

Slow to get started, Taurus always finishes the job, however long it might take – and must not be hurried.

GEMINI

The twin influence is keenly felt. Gemini has a constant need for conversation and communication.

CANCER

Instinctively cautious and protective, the best way forward is to trust those instincts and then act.

LEO

Prepared to take bold decisions and stand their ground, Leo has a track record of creativity in early life.

VIRGO

Order is paramount in organizing not just life, but activities. An interest in physical wellbeing is notable.

LIBRA

Stylish and graceful, life is a quest to find balance and symmetry in everything. Peacekeeping comes naturally.

SCORPIO

Always ready for danger, self-protection is key in their approach to life.

SAGITTARIUS

Travel and a change of scenery are vital. Each new phase of life is marked by change.

CAPRICORN

Organized and methodical, every task in life is undertaken only once due diligence has been paid.

AQUARIUS

Rational and clear-headed, clarity of vision and purpose is the defining quality here.

PISCES

A reluctance to commit to a set path mean that imagination and intuition are important tools to navigate life.

THE SECOND HOUSE
· ·

The Second House is all about all things financial. It concerns itself not just with the money we earn, but all aspects of our financial resources, from our investments to the things we seek to own. In its more abstract form, the Second House is concerned with value, worth, and cost of intangible things as well as material objects.

The Second House controls how we earn our money, how we spend it, our attitude to money, and how it makes us feel. It governs what we own and what we aspire to own. At the same time, it acknowledges that wealth might not just be money in the bank. Spiritual wealth is the resources we build and the sense of values we live our lives by, and these are also governed by the Second House. If all our material wealth disappeared overnight, we would just be left with this – and perhaps that is the key.

PLANETS IN THE SECOND HOUSE

Once we know which planets fall in the second house, we can work out how they influence us. Several planets in a house will emphasize its importance within the birth chart. Below is a list of the main attributes each planet brings.

THE SUN

Money and financial stability are important markers of success. Possessions reflect deep values and an ability to judge the value of things. Practical and persistent, making money comes naturally.

THE MOON

Material security is vital for a sense of emotional wellbeing, and the two are completely connected. Possessions take on an emotional quality and it is important to always have some money in the bank

MERCURY

Communicating, particularly by writing, is a way of earning money. Practical and resourceful, ideas lead to results, including an income stream. Books are highly prized as is anything that places a value on language.

VENUS

Money can buy happiness because it can buy possessions. Venus wants to be surrounded by beautiful things because they bring material pleasure. Fortunately, making money isn't a problem.

MARS

Goal-oriented, acquisitive, and competitive, being rewarded for work with money is what motivates Mars in this house. Being self-sufficient is also very important as is having enough money.

JUPITER

Money flows in thanks to an overabundance of confidence with money. Windfalls happen regularly. The only problem is that spending can overtake earning, so prudence is required.

SATURN

Money is a constant worry, so hard work to earn money is the answer. The amount of money in the bank doesn't matter, it's a question of being self-sufficient and keeping it flowing in to maintain emotional wellbeing.

URANUS

Money comes and goes so regularly it's a real boom-bust situation. Things can change around suddenly, partly because freelance work is often the main source of income.

NEPTUNE

Instinctively capable of earning a lot of money while, simultaneously, naïve enough to be hopeless at saving and easily defrauded, financial affairs are often chaotic and require help.

PLUTO

Money is a means of controlling people and it can become a battleground. A bit too obsessed with possessions, but making money isn't too much of a problem.

ZODIAC SIGNS AND THE SECOND HOUSE

We can further refine our birth charts by looking at the signs the Second House planets sit in, and also the signs on the cusp of the Second House in the chart.

ARIES

Planets in Aries will work to establish security. Aries on the cusp means a self-starter when it comes to finances.

TAURUS

The Second House suits Taurus because it's linked to the gradual accumulation of wealth and its spending.

GEMINI

Money isn't anything Gemini worries about. There might be more than one income stream.

CANCER

Keep an eye on money and possessions coming and going. However, a resourceful approach to finances will keep the money flowing.

LEO

Material possessions are important and help with self-validation. Quality is important and so possessions are always of the best quality.

VIRGO

Thriftiness is the name of the game. Everything is accounted for and saving is what matters.

LIBRA

Good taste and a preference for artisan products mark out Libra's choice of possessions. They are happy to split bills.

SCORPIO

Finances are private and not for public consumption. Boom and bust cycles are commonplace but each time resilience strengthens.

SAGITTARIUS

Spending as and when is what matters. There's no interest in saving or curtailing spending.

CAPRICORN

Hard work, common sense, and financial planning are the order of the day. Everything is noted on a spreadsheet.

AQUARIUS

The intellect matters more than the purse. Where money is concerned, economic equality is what is important, no matter what size the purse is.

PISCES

Over-generous at times to their detriment, Pisceans are slightly clueless when it comes to finances. They won't know how much is in their bank account.

THE THIRD HOUSE

The Third House is dedicated to communication in all its forms in our earliest years. Communication isn't just about how we talk; it's about how we learn, how we build relationships and how we interact with our environment. The mind rules the Third House not just in how we develop language, but the way we communicate our ideas. Early relationships with family members, particularly siblings, and the influence they have on us feature here. Elementary school, the way we learn, and the foundation this provides in life also belong here.

Keeping everything close to home, the Third House also concentrates on how we interact with our local environment and how we move around it. It contrasts with the Ninth House, which is all about far-flung travel.

PLANETS IN THE THIRD HOUSE

Once we know which planets fall in the Third House, we can work out how they influence us. Several planets in a house will emphasize its importance within the birth chart. Below is a list of the main attributes each planet brings.

THE SUN

Both written and spoken communication comes easily because of a natural curiosity and observation skills. Travel and siblings play an important role in our lives.

THE MOON

A skilled communicator, learning comes naturally to this planet. Flexible and endlessly curious, they have a strong bond to their siblings and an ability to bring all kinds of people together.

MERCURY

With a super-agile mind and intellectual curiosity, information is quickly absorbed. A career as a writer or a public speaker is an obvious choice for those with Mercury in their Third House.

VENUS

Learning, travel, and talking are all well represented. Extremely eloquent, their verbal dexterity attracts many admirers. Harmonious relationships with siblings are another bonus.

MARS

Competitive and argumentative, there's no holding back when it comes to speaking out and calling a spade a spade. An independent thinker who will jump to conclusions and is easily distracted.

JUPITER

Intelligent and knowledgeable, there's always something to talk about. Sometimes a filter is needed to get rid of all the junk that's absorbed. Travel, reading, and the company of siblings feature heavily.

SATURN

A deep thinker who takes learning very seriously. Any form of communication is very important. Relationships with siblings are strained at best and sibling rivalry can be an issue.

URANUS

Lightning-fast with an unusual approach that can mean either genius or madness, these people are single-minded, although they can see both points of view in an argument. Sibling relationships are up and down.

NEPTUNE

Intuitive and impressionable and highly sensitive to language. Facts are less important than the feelings they convey. Easily distracted and highly gullible, they are easy prey for their siblings.

PLUTO

With a detective's mind and a desire to solve life's mysteries, learning and language are of paramount significance, along with a heightened sense of privacy.

ZODIAC SIGNS AND THE THIRD HOUSE

We can further refine our birth charts by looking at the signs the Third House planets sit in, and also the signs on the cusp of the Third House in the chart.

ARIES

A quick mind and a readiness to speak their mind. Sibling rivalry is an issue as is the need to compete with them.

TAURUS

Learning is thorough and directed at practical topics, such as how to build a table or grow vegetables.

GEMINI

Able to see patterns where others can't and a good networker, there's an urge to verbalize every thought that pops into their head.

CANCER

There's a preference for non-verbal forms of communication to convey feelings. Protective towards siblings.

LEO

Able to easily communicate thanks to a sound knowledge base, they are confident and bold in their approach.

VIRGO

Everything has to be organized from information to the home. They have a gift for very precise observation.

LIBRA

A diplomatic approach, coupled with an ability to liaise and mediate, means that communications are fair and equal.

SCORPIO

An ability to research and study in great detail any subject that arouses interest plus an uncanny knack to second guess just what is going on.

SAGITTARIUS

Education is about adventure and excitement. An ability to turn even the most mundane into a stimulating possibility.

CAPRICORN

They are practical thinkers who can process information easily and who make sure everything they learn is productive.

AQUARIUS

Learning is about equal opportunities. Rational and with a quirky mind, they seek out like-minded people.

PISCES

Not great at rote learning, they learn through osmosis. Books are a vital escape from the everyday, as is a vivid imagination.

THE FOURTH HOUSE

The Fourth House is both our physical home and our literal home as a place of safety. It is also our living family, our ancestors, and our sense of heritage and lineage.

The concept of home is the place where we actually live as well as a place to withdraw to; it reflects how we see our home. Key to our home is our family. Our immediate family is shown in the Fourth House. It reflects a need to belong and for those who have personal planets in this house a sense of belonging might be significant.

As well as our present family, the Fourth House includes our ancestors, our connection to our homeland and our cultural inheritance as well as a general concept of history. Finally, the Fourth House is concerned with how we find our own inner sanctum.

PLANETS IN THE FOURTH HOUSE

Once we know which planets fall in the Fourth House, we can work out how they influence us. Several planets in a house will emphasize its importance within the birth chart. Below is a list of the main attributes each planet brings.

THE SUN

Home and the family are of central importance, with a strong link to the past and our ancestors. Knowing the past is key to our wellbeing and sense of self.

THE MOON

Emotionally close to family, they place a profound importance on family heritage. The physical home is vital for providing a sense of security, although finding the perfect home might result in many house moves.

MERCURY

Strongly influenced by their parents, home is the center of everything including work. Early life might have involved many house moves. Family heritage is complicated with repercussions that might have to be dealt with.

VENUS

A happy placement means a happy childhood and a particularly close relationship with their mother. Home will be a beautiful, restful place.

MARS

A difficult early home life is compensated for later in life by focusing on their family. They must take care not to create a combative atmosphere at home.

JUPITER

Generous and happy to open their home to others, life improves as they get older. They might travel widely before settling down but whenever that is, they make their home nurturing and comfortable.

SATURN

Family is very important but there is often a feeling of estrangement from one parent in particular. Having their own home is of particular importance to achieve a sense of security.

URANUS

Independent and unconventional, they find it hard to settle down. This could be as a result of a difficult relationship with a parent. Renting rather than buying a home appeals.

NEPTUNE

Family is highly influential, and it is hard to separate from them. There is an ongoing search for the perfect home as a sanctuary. Family members tend to share the same psychic abilities.

PLUTO

One of their parents was so challenging that life is dedicated to dealing with the psychological ramifications. Home is a power base and renovating – whether literal or metaphorical – is key.

ZODIAC SIGNS AND THE FOURTH HOUSE

We can further refine our birth charts by looking at the signs the Fourth House planets sit in, and also the signs on the cusp of the Fourth House in the chart.

ARIES

Early rivalry in the home teaches us how to stand our ground later in life, particularly within the extended family.

TAURUS

Home must be a secure and solid refuge as it is the place where life can slow down and be enjoyed at a more relaxed pace.

GEMINI

The twin might well have two homes or two distinct parts to their family tree, or perhaps even two cultures, which results in split loyalties.

CANCER

They turn a home into a cozy place of security, not just for the family, but for themselves.

LEO

Home is a thing to show off (the more bling the better) and owning a home is an important source of pride.

VIRGO

Everything must be in its place before they can relax. A strong sense of duty means they often take care of their family members.

LIBRA

A belief in sharing and equality comes from early childhood and is vitally important. Often, they take on the role of family mediator.

SCORPIO

A strong bond with their parents, although much family business is never discussed. Home is a place to shut out the rest of the world.

SAGITTARIUS

Home is open to anyone and is often multicultural. Coming from or making a large family is important.

CAPRICORN

Pragmatic and organized, home is somewhere that gives them a firm base from which to operate in the world.

AQUARIUS

Communes and communal living are highly attractive. Friends play as important a role as family in day-to-day life.

PISCES

A house close to water and filled with music helps bring hope and calm. Music and art are as important as the bricks and mortar.

THE FIFTH HOUSE

The Fifth House is all about creativity, entertainment, and romance. It's about the activities we do that bring us joy and help define who we are. This house also includes children as well as risk-taking.

The Fifth House is concerned with creating a legacy of some form, whether it's through our creative impulses, or whether it's through something as physical as the act of having and raising children. It also speaks of our own 'inner child,' the part of us that we keep hidden but which brings us pleasure. It is about realizing the value of reinforcing the life spirit by allowing us to indulge ourselves.

Romance features and the Fifth House might show how we like to show love to those closest to us, as well as how we like to be made to feel. It's all about what brings passion to us and makes us feel special. We might put our heart on the line for love, which is why gambling and risk-taking appear in this house. It covers both literal and metaphorical risks.

PLANETS IN THIS HOUSE

Once we know which planets fall in the Fifth House, we can work out how they influence us. Several planets in a house will emphasize its importance within the birth chart. Below is a list of the main attributes each planet brings.

THE SUN

A natural attention and pleasure seeker, the spotlight is where they prefer to be. Happiness can be found in any creative outlet including children, romance, and artistic pursuits.

THE MOON

Dramatic and emotional, their needs have to be center stage. They are creative, talented, and romantic and share a special bond with children, whether they are their own or not.

MERCURY

Telling stories, perhaps for a living, shows the importance of communication to these creative thinkers. They love to speculate and need a partner who fires them up intellectually.

VENUS

Love and romance are vital in any relationship, as is the need to be admired. That's not a problem as they attract people, especially children. Everyone wants to be their friend.

MARS

Competitive with a love of playing games, they are impulsive risk-takers who love creating new projects, whether it's children or work. They define themselves by their high sex drive.

JUPITER

This placement is about having fun no matter what. Romance features highly, as does play. Those who become parents love the whole family thing, especially those family vacations.

SATURN

Everything is serious here. It's hard to lighten up, and even creative pastimes involve games like chess. Creativity is important, but the fear of failure can stifle it. Dating involves older, more serious partners.

URANUS

A constant flow of ideas means that creative impulses might never happen because one idea follows another. Love affairs are impulsive and break-ups frequent. Children might seem to limit their freedom.

NEPTUNE

Creative but with a tendency not to focus, it can be hard for this placement to settle. In love affairs, they are attracted to platonic relationships and secret affairs. If they can commit to a family, they share a psychic bond.

PLUTO

Romance is an obsession. Having children or another creative outlet is all-encompassing. Power struggles are common with children and gambling is addictive.

ZODIAC SIGNS AND THE FIFTH HOUSE

We can further refine our birth charts by looking at the signs the Fifth House planets sit in, and also the signs on the cusp of the Fifth House in the chart.

ARIES

Risk taking appeals. Any sport that comes with a hint of danger is attractive – it's a good way of burning up all their energy.

TAURUS

Making things, such as pots, appeals; anything that has a tangible quality. Sensuousness is part of romance.

GEMINI

A love affair is all about a meeting of minds, and intellectual compatibility trumps physical attraction.

CANCER

Taking care of their family is what motivates them. Being close to the sea helps their creativity.

LEO

Being creative is synonymous with the joy and meaning that life brings. In love, Leo is always warm-hearted.

VIRGO

Accuracy and precision in everything they do can stifle the creative urge. A working vacation is more relaxing than a vacation.

LIBRA

Anything creative must be well-designed and beautiful to look at as perfection is the ultimate goal. They are attracted to classically attractive people.

SCORPIO

Loyalty and passion define romance, although jealousy is also often a feature. There's a sting in the tail with their sense of humor.

SAGITTARIUS

Vacations have to be long-lasting and activities such as archery and marathon running appeal more than team sports.

CAPRICORN

Risk-taking isn't in their nature. They will only take calculated risks. A sense of duty pervades everything they do.

AQUARIUS

An awareness of how different they are only increases their sense of being special. Romance tends to grow from friendship.

PISCES

Romance is all about being transported; this is a double-edged sword as it often leads to disappointment.

THE SIXTH HOUSE

This is the house that deals with the everyday; it's concerned with work and chores that have to be done. Daily routines, obligations, and duties and all the things needed to pay the bills and keep life ticking over.

The Sixth House deals with our working lives; it shows us how we deal with the grind of the everyday and how we can better deal with our feelings to make it as enjoyable as possible. It acknowledges the importance of chores and duties in our daily lives, because without them, daily life would seize up.

Health features in the Sixth House. Physical routines keep our bodies working well, and this house shows which exercise we are best suited to. This house also deals with the relationships we have with those we work for or who work for us.

PLANETS IN THE SIXTH HOUSE

Once we know which planets fall in the Sixth House, we can work out how they influence us. Several planets in a house will emphasize its importance within the birth chart. Below is a list of the main attributes each planet brings.

THE SUN

Work is a vital focus because it is how they define themselves. They worry about their health, usually unnecessarily. No matter what their Sun sign, they are perfectionists.

THE MOON

Working just for money is never going to be enough. They have to enjoy their work and feel fulfilled. They need to keep in touch with their feelings to ensure their health stays good.

MERCURY

Work has to be satisfying because they allow it to take over their lives. Slightly nervous, they worry constantly about their health to the point of hypochondria.

VENUS

Work is as crucial to their wellbeing as love. They often meet their partners and friends through work. Popular, they are often used to mediate office disputes. Fulfilling work makes them happy and improves their health.

MARS

They want work to challenge them, and they are happy to take a gamble. Efficient and precise, the less of a routine the better. Daily physical exercise is key to their mental wellbeing.

JUPITER

In the right job, they will put in all the hours required. There's a tendency to overwork, and they aren't too fussy about details. Excess is a problem for work and health – and should be avoided.

SATURN

Reliable and diligent, they take their work very seriously. They need a career that is satisfying. In daily life, they pay the same attention to chores. Health is a constant worry, so regular check-ups are a good idea.

URANUS

Nine-to-five isn't for them. The unpredictability of freelance work suits better. The more unusual the job, the better. Health-wise, they favor alternative therapies over conventional medicine.

NEPTUNE

Surroundings matter at work; a job outdoors preferably close to the sea would be ideal. Intuition serves them well, particularly when it comes to health issues and they will consult alternative practitioners.

PLUTO

Focused, they can work obsessively in their quest for power. Often, they have healing qualities and they need to do a job that means something, otherwise their health will suffer.

ZODIAC SIGNS AND THE SIXTH HOUSE

We can further refine our birth charts by looking at the signs the Sixth House planets sit in, and also the signs on the cusp of the Sixth House in the chart.

ARIES

They set themselves lots of goals each working day and achieve them. Housework is done in a flash.

TAURUS

Methodical, a slow working pace best suits Taurus. They need to pay attention to their body's needs.

GEMINI

They keep themselves busy at work and at home – and this suits their personality. They love working out how things work.

CANCER

Getting along with coworkers so they are one big happy family is important, and they love to mother them.

LEO

They define themselves through their work, and so it's important that it reflects their talents and capabilities.

VIRGO

Happy to work in the background, they get on with all the boring chores. They need to keep a close eye on their diet.

LIBRA

A harmonious workplace is key, and playing the diplomat in the office is second nature. Keeping everything in balance physically brings a sense of wellbeing.

SCORPIO

Typically, they work in bursts of intense activity, followed by rest both in the office and completing their daily tasks.

SAGITTARIUS

Freedom in daily life and in the workplace is vital, as is a shared sense of humor with coworkers.

CAPRICORN

It is crucial to their sense of self that work is all done properly, and no detail has been missed. They appreciate efficient systems.

AQUARIUS

Equality among fellow workers is a prerequisite and they will often look to work among a community of likeminded people.

PISCES

Timekeeping isn't their strength as they have their own daily rhythm. They avoid daily chores, but need them to give the day a structure.

THE SEVENTH HOUSE

Relationships are the domain of the Seventh House. Any kind of
relationship is included in this house, from marriages to disputes to
business partnerships. Think about any kind of relationship between
people.

The Seventh House is the house that is concerned with marriage or any
kind of contractual partnership, whether it is to cement a relationship
or escape from one. This house will play a part in any decision.
Similarly, it is the house of litigation; where enemies fight out their
battles and conflict is settled.

Another area of interest for the Seventh House is the 'other.' By this we
mean the elements that make each person feel whole. It might be that we
think our missing attributes are found in other people when, in fact, they
are to be found within us. The Seventh House will help to find them.

PLANETS IN THE SEVENTH HOUSE

Once we know which planets fall in the Seventh House, we can work
out how they influence us. Several planets in a house will emphasize its
importance within the birth chart. Below is a list of the main attributes
each planet brings.

THE SUN

Relationships, be they marriage or other partnerships, are key to their
sense of identity, but they vacillate between commitment and being
alone. Within any relationship, they need to find their sense of self.

THE MOON

Relationships are vitally important to their happiness but there is always a danger that having made the decision to commit, they become glorified doormats. Their sensitivity is very attractive to others.

MERCURY

Sociable, they crave conversation and intellectual stimulation. They find it easy to get on with people, but are easily bored and often don't like commitment. Once they find an intellectual equal, the conversation never stops.

VENUS

Happiest when they are in a relationship, their innate charm means they attract a wide group of people. Business relationships also flourish because they are so easy to get along with.

MARS

Relationships are another area in which combative Mars fights for supremacy. When things aren't going well, they are quick to confront the issues meaning kiss and make-up has a special place in this house.

JUPITER

Easy to get along with and very sociable, this placement means that they have lots of opportunities to create long-lasting relationships in every part of their lives. Divorce is rare.

SATURN

If they can overcome their fears about intimacy, theirs is a serious approach to marriage. Often, they are attracted to an older person who is responsible and with whom they can have a long-lasting relationship.

URANUS

They will only commit if they find somebody who is willing to allow them their freedom. Often, they marry in haste and can divorce equally fast. The more unconventional their partner, the better.

NEPTUNE

A desire for the perfect partner means that idealism often gets in the way of realism when they are looking for their spiritual soulmate. Added to that, their preference for artistic, moody people can be a recipe for trouble.

PLUTO

They tend to pick domineering partners both in love and business. It is hard for them to keep a clear vision of self in such circumstances as they are easily influenced by their partners.

ZODIAC SIGNS AND THE SEVENTH HOUSE

We can further refine our birth charts by looking at the signs the Seventh House planets sit in, and also the signs on the cusp of the Seventh House in the chart.

ARIES

In relationships, they can adopt an aggressive stance which is complemented with Libra rising by a desire for fairness.

TAURUS

Stability and loyalty are key qualities they look for in any relationship. This balances Scorpio rising's intense approach.

GEMINI

Humor and variety are key requirements in any relationship. They learn to articulate Sagittarius rising's view of the world.

CANCER

A desire for a family helps determine which partner they choose. They are more sentimental than their Capricorn rising would suggest.

LEO

Their Aquarian rising means they seek out praise and attention more than might be expected. Relationships show how special they are.

VIRGO

Relationships provide the practical balance to the dreamy, poetic qualities that Pisces rising bring to them.

LIBRA

Aggressive Aries rising is challenged by the need to compromise. Relationships encourage a fair-minded approach.

SCORPIO

Passionate and intense in any relationship, which might come as a surprise as placid Taurus rises in this sign.

SAGITTARIUS

Other people are fascinating and help find meaning in the information garnered by Gemini rising.

CAPRICORN

Any relationship must provide stability to balance the constant stream of feelings from their Cancer rising.

AQUARIUS

In relationships, they are more democratic than their Leo rising might suggest. Freedom is key to any relationship.

PISCES

Virgo rising's practical skills assist in their helping of others. Romantic relationships can take them to another level.

THE EIGHTH HOUSE

The Eighth House deals with all the things that lie below the surface and much that makes up the darker side of life, such as death and loss. It also covers the murky and often complex issue of shared finance.

If the last house was all about contracts and relationships, the Eighth House moves into the area of what lies beneath those contracts and relationships. It deals with all the unspoken contracts, power control, and deep intimacies that make up relationships. Within that are things that go beyond our control, such as loss and death. What links them is the powerful emotions they arouse within us.

Fortunately, the Eighth House also deals with our ability for regeneration and growth out of despair and tragedy. When it comes to financial matters, this house covers an area of both trust and mistrust, of debt and financial obligation, which makes it a potential minefield.

PLANETS IN THE EIGHTH HOUSE

Once we know which planets fall in the Eighth House, we can work out how they influence us. Several planets in a house will emphasize its importance within the birth chart. Below is a list of the main attributes each planet brings.

THE SUN

Deeply emotional and deep thinking, their life's focus is to better understand their deepest psyche. This can be through intimate relationships. Sex along with money, particularly legacies, play an important role.

THE MOON

Their intuition and sensitivity mean they can help themselves and others to heal emotional wounds. Emotionally literate, they face reality. Finances can be more of a challenge.

MERCURY

A penetrating mind gives them the extraordinary capabilities when it comes to research and an unerring ability to learn secrets and get to the bottom of any situation.

VENUS

A slave to their feelings and libido, their love lives are invariably complicated. They are very good with money and often gain it not through work, but through marriage, inheritance, or smart investing.

MARS

Drawn to adventure, they are fearless in any situation, which many others find attractive. Interested in financial wheeling and dealing, shared finances can be a source of conflict.

JUPITER

Able to withstand almost anything and with excellent recovery powers, they not only survive but support others. Financially, they can gain from a variety of sources including insurance and investments.

SATURN

Capable of great insights, they need to overcome their fear of death and deal with their sexual issues. They are great with money, which comes in handy as their partners are often poor with it.

URANUS

A bit of distance is needed in emotional relationships because there are so many. Equally good with money, they are canny investors. Metaphysical subjects interest them.

NEPTUNE

Any kind of extrasensory communication attracts them. Sometimes they trust their intuition too much and need to be wary when it comes to money, especially with a business partner.

PLUTO

Intuitive, perceptive, and fascinated by the big topics in life, their survival instincts can often be tested in difficult relationships and in financial losses.

ZODIAC SIGNS AND THE EIGHTH HOUSE

We can further refine our birth charts by looking at the signs the Eighth House planets sit in, and also the signs on the cusp of the Eighth House in the chart.

ARIES

They tend to act first and think later. This can have repercussions in their love lives or with investments they make.

TAURUS

By being sensible, they ride any financial storm and have a knack for turning a profit.

GEMINI

Intimacy is about the meeting of minds. They are always curious to know what motivates people.

CANCER

They are very private people who are highly in tune with their emotional wellbeing, which helps them stay grounded.

LEO

They have the Midas touch when it comes to investing their money, and they like to take charge of any joint finances.

VIRGO

Good in a crisis, it takes them some time to process difficult experiences, but they do so calmly and wisely.

LIBRA

Everything in a relationship must be split evenly and fairly, including finances.

SCORPIO

They fall hard and intensely for their partners, and the more they give of themselves, the more committed they become. Money can be a bone of contention.

SAGITTARIUS

They like to take risks financially. Relationships are an adventure that allow them to learn more.

CAPRICORN

Keeping finances separate in a relationship is important. It can be hard for them to commit deeply in a relationship.

AQUARIUS

Able to sort the real from the unreal is their skill. In any relationship, they need to keep a modicum of freedom.

PISCES

Deep intimacy is a means to make life extraordinary, and they willingly give their all to their partner.

THE NINTH HOUSE

The Ninth House is concerned with all things to do with travel, both physical and metaphorical. It also covers ethical and legal issues, and the bigger questions life poses.

This house tries to answer life's fundamental questions of the morals and ethics by which we choose to live our lives. So, the law, philosophy, and politics are all covered by the Ninth House. Coupled with this is a deeper learning. While the Third House was about early-life learning, this house looks beyond the facts to a more profound learning.

Journeys in all their forms belong in the Ninth House. It is unfamiliar territory, which helps us to a greater understanding of ourselves, be it learning something new or physically exploring somewhere new.

PLANETS IN THE NINTH HOUSE

Once we know which planets fall in the Ninth House, we can work out how they influence us. Several planets in a house will emphasize its importance within the birth chart. Below is a list of the main attributes each planet brings.

THE SUN

Both travel and education are fundamental to giving their life its true meaning. Gaining knowledge in any form gives them confidence to create their own philosophy of life.

THE MOON

With an active imagination and a desire for new things, they push the boundaries of life, making themselves happier in the process. Eager to explore different cultures and philosophies until one chimes, they use travel to nurture their souls.

MERCURY

A life-long love of learning that encompasses grappling with new ideas, traveling to new lands and meeting new people is what motivates those with this placement. Working in education is an ideal career.

VENUS

They embrace anything, which allows them to expand their horizons. Excited by ideas and complex thought processes, they find beauty in everything they study. Other cultures stimulate them.

MARS

An independent thinker and intrepid explorer into the unknown, they carve out a path others will follow. Motivated by ideas thrown up by their interest in law, religion, and education, their obsessive nature needs to be reined in at times.

JUPITER

A natural teacher, they want to learn as much as possible about as many subjects as is possible and spread the knowledge. Anything that expands their horizons is a hit; faith is important as is travel.

SATURN

Everything they do is carefully considered. They love to explore profound ideas, particularly in philosophy and religion. Travel and anything that involves the unknown is only undertaken when all preparations have been made.

URANUS

Unusual and unorthodox ideas are what attracts this placement. A desire for enlightenment follows their own way of looking at the world in fields as varied as travel and education.

NEPTUNE

Spiritual journeys and visions belong to Neptune here because the Ninth House is the house of prophecy. Before they find their spiritual path, Neptune will take many different directions.

PLUTO

Education and travel are the key to self-transformation. Studying and immersing themselves in other cultures helps to deepen their understanding. They are particularly interested in philosophy, religion, and the law.

ZODIAC SIGNS AND THE NINTH HOUSE

We can further refine our birth charts by looking at the signs the Ninth House planets sit in, and also the signs on the cusp of the Ninth House in the chart.

ARIES

They love to visit offbeat places, particularly on their own. They will always forge their own path and won't be held back.

TAURUS

A love of luxury characterizes their approach to travel. They approach any kind of learning in a methodical and patient way.

GEMINI

Endlessly curious, they love to study and learn. They are able to explain things concisely and simply however complex the ideas behind them are.

CANCER

They study whatever grabs their fancy and moves them. Foreign cultures hold great appeal.

LEO

Traveling is an important route to personal growth, but it has to be done in style! Going outside their comfort zone will help their sense of identity.

VIRGO

It is only with a backup plan worked through and every contingency planned for that they set off on their travels.

LIBRA

Equality defines how they see their moral code. They are interested in subjects as diverse as fashion and social sciences.

SCORPIO

Philosophical questions fascinate them, and they will take their studies to the next level in an effort to answer questions that fascinate them.

SAGITTARIUS

Adventure is what drives them, and they see learning and the world as borderless and unrestricted.

CAPRICORN

They approach learning and teaching in a business-like manner, and they are keen to acquire qualifications.

AQUARIUS

More interested in how they might help their community than themselves, they steer their learning and teaching in that direction.

PISCES

Fired by their imagination, they long for faraway lands and mystery destinations as an escape from real life.

THE TENTH HOUSE

The image that we present to the world is what the Tenth House is all about. It is about the jobs we do, our professional achievements and success, and our role within the world at large.

The Tenth House is all about peaks; about aiming for the peak of our careers and for the peak of our ambition. It is concerned with how we achieve our best self through work and how we present that self to the world. The profession we choose shows the world what matters to us.

Finally, the Tenth House represents the different authority figures who have influenced and still influence us, from our parents to our bosses at work, and how we learn from them.

PLANETS IN THE TENTH HOUSE

Once we know which planets fall in the Tenth House, we can work out how they influence us. Several planets in a house will emphasize its importance within the birth chart. Below is a list of the main attributes each planet brings.

THE SUN

Work is vitally important to them. Their leadership skills and determination to succeed means that a job in which they can take a leading role is the best fit, and will likely lead to professional success.

THE MOON

Professional success only matters if it combines with peace of mind that they have a career that matters. Once they find that career, they will work endlessly to be successful. It could be being a full-time parent or a foster parent.

MERCURY

Communication is key to a stimulating career, perhaps as a writer, because this placement values articulate and clever people above everything. The ideal job must have variety; if not, they will change jobs frequently.

VENUS

Outgoing and popular, they are skilled at bringing people together. A career in the arts suits them best, and they will find people willing to help them up the career ladder. They need to look their best at work.

MARS

Determined to be the boss, they like *grands projets* – any large-scale career that requires intelligence, ambition, and drive. They want a career that excites them, and they don't mind a bit of fame on the side.

JUPITER

They aim high because they want a career with room for improvement and recognition. With natural leadership qualities and charisma, people want to help them. Being famous suits them down to the ground.

SATURN

Willing to take on a lot of responsibility, they are ambitious and persistent. They will most likely get to the top through hard work, but that's alright with them. Partly, this is to show their dad just how capable they are.

URANUS

Probably best suited to the freelance world, bowing to authority is not going to happen with this placement. Any career that allows full independence is to be considered. Their original way of looking at the world means opportunities appear from unexpected places.

NEPTUNE

They need a career that allows them to use their intuition and imagination. Any practical career will be a waste of time. Consider a career in the arts. Asserting themselves can be a real issue.

PLUTO

Often successful, they reject authority figures and wish to hold all the power themselves. It might take them some time to get power but once they do, they are the real deal.

ZODIAC SIGNS AND THE TENTH HOUSE

We can further refine our birth charts by looking at the signs the Tenth House planets sit in, and also the signs on the cusp of the Tenth House in the chart.

ARIES

A natural self-starter, they work hard to get ahead and show just what they are capable of. In the office, they want to be the boss.

TAURUS

A steady climb and a willingness to stick out a job for years characterizes the practical Taurus's approach to work.

GEMINI

Any career path may well have two parts to it, and this keeps them interested and ambitious. They want to be seen as intelligent.

CANCER

Nurturing features heavily in career choices, and belonging to a professional family is important. Instinct and intuition serve them well.

LEO

Public image is vital to their sense of self, and they are not slow to promote themselves on the journey to the top of the career ladder.

VIRGO

Creative fields and anything that involves precision or making order will appeal to the logic of Virgo.

LIBRA

In any career they want to be seen to be fair and even-handed. Anything that involves diplomacy and bridge-building suits them well.

SCORPIO

Hard work and determination mark out their work careers. A job that needs passion and commitment suits them best.

SAGITTARIUS

The sky's the limit where work is concerned. International and educational aspects of any job are particularly appealing.

CAPRICORN

A traditional career with a professional qualification most appeals. Add to that a job that requires good organizational and administrative skills, and it's the perfect career.

AQUARIUS

The best job is one that involves working in a team with like-minded people. They are always approachable and inclusive, no matter what job they do.

PISCES

With no clear direction, it might take a while to find the right career. But, one that uses their compassion and creativity would be the best fit.

THE ELEVENTH HOUSE
· ·

Friendship and any kind of social network are housed in the Eleventh House. The planets tell us the position we occupy in our many network groups.

The Fifth House is the house of play and this house is its playground. It is where we make the time and space to spend time with our friends and acquaintances. It is a positive place where those who have our best interests at heart can be found. Our contribution is one of participation in any kind of group activity from being a member of a club to perhaps something larger.

The Eleventh House is also concerned with the future and our attitude towards planning for it so that we can make our dreams and plans a reality. Within that is how we view society and how much of a personal contribution we are prepared to make to improve the future for everyone.

PLANETS IN THE ELEVENTH HOUSE

Once we know which planets fall in the Eleventh House, we can work out how they influence us. Several planets in a house will emphasize its importance within the birth chart. Below is a list of the main attributes each planet brings.

THE SUN

Friends play a huge role in their life and they may define themselves through those friendships. They have high ideals and belonging to a community gives them a sense of purpose and wellbeing.

THE MOON

Outgoing and popular, they have a wide circle of friends. As a nurturer, people flock to them. Aspirations and goals change through life and with them, friendship groups may alter.

MERCURY

A busy social life is vital to their well-being. They make friends easily but, depending on the alignment of other planets, these friendships might be temporary. A networker, they prefer to work in a group.

VENUS

With a charming and affectionate nature, they are the center of any social group as people naturally gravitate to them. They inspire devotion and are equally devoted.

MARS

Their competitive nature is never far from the surface when they are with friends and acquaintances, and they can behave unreasonably. A natural leader, they fight for social or political causes.

JUPITER

Well-loved and easy to get along with, they work well with any group and have tons of friends. The more ambitious the plans, the better, particularly with group activities.

SATURN

Setting the bar high, they don't make friends easily, but those they do make will be friends for life. Ambitious, they are great organizers and can make things happen when they get people together.

URANUS

With a wide range of interests, the friends they acquire reflect their scattered interests. Friends come and go, particularly those who work with them on whatever cause is close to their heart.

NEPTUNE

They see the best in people and are happy to sacrifice their own desires for the greater cause. This, however, isn't always a wise move. They need to perhaps be a bit more discriminating.

PLUTO

Friends help shape who they become, and many of the best experiences in life come through those friendships. Many of these friendships are particularly intense.

ZODIAC SIGNS AND THE ELEVENTH HOUSE

We can further refine our birth charts by looking at the signs the Eleventh House planets sit in, and also the signs on the cusp of the Eleventh House in the chart.

ARIES

A busy social life is a must, but they like to keep their independence within the group and with their friends.

TAURUS

They expect loyalty from their friends, which they return in spades. Friends are for the long-term.

GEMINI

A love of socializing and a need for networking characterize Gemini. They love to talk with their wide social group.

CANCER

Friends are like family, and the more the merrier. Society for them is about nurturing and supporting one another.

LEO

They like to take charge of their social groups, where they are the center of attention. Leo happily gives up their time and attention for others.

VIRGO

Being a valued part of any group is reward enough for Virgo. They are more concerned about the group's wellbeing than their own.

LIBRA

Often they have to mediate between their friends because of their innate sense of fairness and harmony.

SCORPIO

Friendship is about longevity, intensity, and passion. It is never a frivolous enterprise.

SAGITTARIUS

Meeting people from different cultures is as important as it is exciting for their general wellbeing.

CAPRICORN

Serious, they like to take control of any social group. They might end up being elected leader because of their maturity.

AQUARIUS

They believe that everyone is equal, and it is important that everyone they know is treated the same.

PISCES

Sensitive and sympathetic with all their friends, they love belonging to a community because it brings out their altruistic side.

TWELFTH HOUSE

The Twelfth and final House is about release and a completion of the cycle. It represents our unconscious secrets and where we not only make sacrifices, but also show our devotion and our selflessness.

The Twelfth House is an otherworldly house. For some astrologers it is where prisons and hospitals are located; those institutions that are on the periphery of everyday life. It is also where religious retreats are located, and, as such, the house contains within it the concept of universal love, charity, and compassion as a gift to the world.

It is the house of escape and withdrawal, and ultimately the house of transcendence. It is where we leave the wheel of life, for however long, in order to reach a state of bliss.

PLANETS IN THE TWELFTH HOUSE

Once we know which planets fall in the Twelfth House, we can work out how they influence us. Several planets in a house will emphasize its importance within the birth chart. Below is a list of the main attributes each planet brings.

THE SUN

A sense of identity might come to those who choose to dedicate themselves to public service. Secretive and intuitive, they nourish their souls with spiritual activity. A lover of solitude, they nevertheless make great actors.

THE MOON

With a tendency to withdraw from the world, they are moody and secretive, and seek solace in clandestine relationships. Institutions feature as places where they can do as much good to themselves as to others.

MERCURY

They are secretive, intuitive, and mysterious, and look for meaning in dreams. Creative thinking is a must as is solitude. The spiritual and intangible attracts them.

VENUS

Highly sensitive and hyper aware of others' feelings, they need their privacy and can often fall into illicit love affairs in their quest for the non-existent perfect lover. Solitude is essential for their soul.

MARS

Much of their true nature is kept hidden, meaning they do not think people truly 'get' them. An effective fighter for those who are more vulnerable, they need their own space to thrive.

JUPITER

Generous and sympathetic, they tend to overextend themselves and need downtime to recalibrate. They love others' company, especially when it involves exploring the world.

SATURN

Beneath their calm and efficient exterior is a seething turmoil of fear and pessimism. They work well alone but hate it, and they hate being alone, but it's essential for their mental health.

URANUS

Unconventional, they prize their freedom above everything and will rebel against convention. Their intuition means they are often one step ahead of everyone else, and can spot a trend long before the rest of us.

NEPTUNE

Highly attuned to their unconscious, they are deeply connected to their dreams, secrets, and the otherness of life. Empathetic, they will help anyone in need to the detriment of themselves.

PLUTO

By delving into their own unconscious, they can bring about great changes. They keep their own power and strength hidden, but when they employ both, they have the capacity to transform lives.

ZODIAC SIGNS AND THE TWELFTH HOUSE

We can further refine our birth charts by looking at the signs the Twelfth House planets sit in, and also the signs on the cusp of the Twelfth House in the chart.

ARIES

Charity work appeals, especially when they can bring their initiative and energy to the cause.

TAURUS

Spending time in nature brings a sense of wellbeing and relaxation that is hard for Taurus to find anywhere else.

GEMINI

They love to use their intellect to study the world of the imagination in all its complexity, and they bring great clarity.

CANCER

They work hard behind the scenes to look after those who can't look after themselves. Their home is a sanctuary.

LEO

Being adored matters to Leo, who works hard to impress and to leave no one in doubt of their abilities.

VIRGO

They are happy to perform those little practical acts which make life so much better, and they don't expect any praise in return.

LIBRA

Romantic relationships matter to Libra, but if trust is broken, they should see this as an opportunity to grow and develop.

SCORPIO

Strongly intuitive, they are suspicious of anything that is hidden from view and take an interest in the mystical.

SAGITTARIUS

They willingly travel into the unknown and like to get as far away as possible.

CAPRICORN

They distrust anything they cannot see or prove. They bring structure and purpose to anything that is liminal.

AQUARIUS

A scientific explanation exists for most mysteries, and Aquarius likes to find them. They like to escape on a regular basis.

PISCES

Highly sensitive to feelings and moods, they need to lay down boundaries, so they don't absorb everyone else's worries.

ASTROLOGICAL
INFLUENCES
· ·

Now we have considered the main features of astrology, let's take it to the next level and look at some more elements that can help add the personal details onto our horoscopes and birth charts. These personal details help to refine horoscopes and make them more accurate.

We will consider our Moon sign, which, as the name suggests, is the sign the Moon sat in at birth. Then, we will look at our Ascendant or rising sign. This is often the most difficult part of casting a chart because it requires knowing the exact time of birth. To work out ascendants, the charts work in two-hour increments. As long as we are fairly accurate about when we were born, we can calculate our rising sign. In most cases, our rising sign will be different from our Sun and Moon signs. Astrologers believe that if the signs are the same, life is much more straightforward because there is no conflict within the signs.

Another astrological term that is sometimes used is 'cusp.' Cusp is used in two ways in astrology. People can be born on the cusp; that means their birthday falls at the end of one sign and the beginning of another, which means that they may well have qualities from both signs. The cusp of a house, which is the other use, means the starting point of a house.

Finally, we will consider that astrology might seem to suggest that there's no room for free will. That would be to misunderstand the aim of astrology, which, as we have seen, is to guide us towards a better understanding of ourselves.

MOON SIGNS

Looking at the sky from Earth, the Moon and the Sun appear to be the same size. We know from science that is wrong, however, in astrology, they have always been and still are treated as equals, or partners. Where the Sun represents our conscious self and basic essence, the Moon, thanks to its many phases, represents our many moods, our varying emotional responses and our unconscious self.

The sign that the Moon occupied at our birth describes our emotional life. Just as the Moon waxes and wanes, so do our emotions throughout the month. This can be particularly true for people who experience monthly menstruation cycles. The Moon sign shows us what gives us a sense of home and security – what we need to feel safe, secure, and comfortable. It also drives some of our gut instincts and how we respond on a primal level.

Since the Moon comes out at night, the Moon sign influences the parts of ourselves which only become visible during a period of self-reflection or vulnerability. Often, it doesn't present externally or immediately like the Sun sign or Ascendant, but it becomes much more visible as we get to know a person and see how they respond to different life situations.

To work out where the Moon is in our birth chart, we need to know our exact time of birth. Unlike the Sun, the Moon moves into a new sign every two to three days. If it moved from one sign to the next on the actual birthdate, knowing the precise time of birth is essential. Online charts make it easy to look up. Remember to allow for different time zones as many sites are American.

For some lucky souls, their Sun and Moon signs are the same. It makes life easier for them; if their Sun sign is Capricorn with all its focus on steady reliability, we can see that having a Capricorn Moon sign makes for a much easier life than say a dreamy Pisces Moon sign. Everything will be in sync – their conscious and unconscious selves, their needs and their desires. For the rest of us, and that's a lot of us, clashing Moon and Sun signs are just the way it is, and we have to accept it.

THE MOON IN EACH SIGN

ARIES

The Moon in Aries creates pioneers who tend to act impulsively without thinking through the consequences. They are easily frustrated and angered, which is not surprising since Mars, the planet of aggression and war, rules Aries. Passionate, competitive, and argumentative, they like to be first in everything they do. No shrinking violet, they want recognition. Aries Moon signs are courageous; they champion any cause or person they believe in. They prize their independence and freedom within any relationship; being tied down terrifies them.

TAURUS

Lasting luxury is essential for Taurus Moon signs. Since Venus, the planet of beauty and decadence rules Taurus, this makes sense. A Taurus Moon sign will invest time and effort in all their relationships, romantic or platonic, which is why they last and why they so rarely make mistakes. The only downside is that slow-moving Taurus can get too comfortable surrounded by all their luxury and become a tad lazy.

GEMINI

The sign of the twins and a flighty air sign to boot, a Gemini Moon sign can find it hard to make decisions and commit. Great ones for weighing up all the options, they are reluctant to put their money where their mouth is. They also find it hard to let their emotions in; they are too busy rationalizing them. This can lead to them suffering from restlessness, judgmental behavior, and even depression. Close friends are vital to act as a sounding board for them.

CANCER

A cozy home life appeals most to the Cancer Moon sign. Highly sensitive and attuned to others' needs, they do anything to nurture their loved ones. Motherhood is associated with Cancer, and those born with a Cancer Moon sign have close bonds to their mothers – and can become devoted mothers themselves. The Moon sign makes them highly creative and a home-loving, sensitive, and nurturing being. All they ask is for a little appreciation, otherwise they can become a bit moody.

LEO

A Leo Moon sign loves nothing more than the limelight. They want to be adored and to adore in return. They are creative creatures who love to perform, sometimes blurring the line between the stage and real life. But, if we ignore the dramatics, a Leo Moon sign will be kind, honest, and generous. They make the best friends because of their loyalty and their non-stop ability to keep us entertained. If Leo can be kept away from its ego-mania, the Moon sign leaves others feeling better about themselves.

VIRGO

Those born with a Virgo Moon sign possess an innate readiness to put others first, and to help them in constructive and supportive ways. They keep their emotions closely guarded while happily helping friends through any crisis. To live at ease, a Virgo Moon sign needs order in their lives as they are obsessively tidy. They watch their weight and make sure they exercise. Everything they do reflects their need to be in control. The only problem is that this constant quest for perfection can make them a bit too obsessive. They need to relax just a bit.

LIBRA

Like those born with their Sun in Libra, a Libra Moon sign just wants peace, love, and harmony. They are looking for their soulmate, the person who will complete them by balancing their qualities. Diplomatic by nature, it is hard for a Libra Moon sign to declare a winner in an argument, partly because they can always see both sides and partly because they hate to offend anyone. They will do anything to keep the peace. Ruled by Venus, they love beauty and need to take care not to overspend on gorgeous things.

SCORPIO

A Scorpio Moon sign is intense! They need to feel loved and with a partner, sexual chemistry is a must – as is passion and desire. Highly suspicious, Scorpio Moon signs need proof of trust from others before they give them their loyalty. It is hard to please a Scorpio Moon sign. However, when things work, they develop such a deep bond that anything is possible. They operate well in any crisis, and the only drawback is that they find it hard to say how they really feel.

SAGITTARIUS

Just like those born with their Sun in Sagittarius, the Sagittarius Moon sign is adventurous and obsessed with their freedom. They hate to feel claustrophobic. But when they do commit to a relationship, they'll stick around for the long haul. Ruled by Jupiter, a Sagittarius Moon sign seeks wisdom and truth. As a fire sign, Sagittarius Moon individuals can get angry when they feel others are being provincial and narrow-minded; for them the world is one of infinite possibility, which they want to explore.

CAPRICORN

Those born under a Capricorn Moon sign are not only highly ambitious leaders, but they are happy to shoulder responsibility. They expect success and accolades, but at the expense of their own wants and desires. While they're dependable, a Capricorn Moon sign can feel resentful about putting duty before desire. Another issue for them is facing their feelings and asking for what they really want. Stubborn by nature, they might hesitate to enter or leave a relationship due to feeling obliged. Patience is crucial when dealing with those born with a Capricorn Moon.

AQUARIUS

Aquarius Moon signs always have one foot in the future. They are experimental and avant-garde, and are always on the look-out for the latest thing, even if they don't really enjoy it. Quirky, they attract all kinds of people, and enjoy being footloose and fancy-free. This might be because they are not very good at expressing how they really feel about things. Aquarius Moon signs tend to mix pushing boundaries with an urge to rationalize everything.

PISCES

People born with a Pisces Moon sign take mysteriousness to a new level, not just for those around them, but for themselves. They are all about emotion although, strangely, they struggle to articulate their feelings. Moon signs tend to attract people needing help; their challenge is to learn when to say no. A Pisces Moon sign – symbolized by the two fishes swimming in opposite directions – needs others to accept the ups and downs of their constantly changing moods and allow them to be emotionally vulnerable. They want to feel needed, which makes them the most trustworthy of friends.

ASCENDANTS AND DESCENDANTS

ASCENDANTS

Also known as the rising sign, the Ascendant is the furthest left point of the central horizon line and reveals which Zodiac sign was emerging from the eastern horizon at our exact moment of birth.

Our Ascendant is our mask; it's the surface of our personality and the image we project to others. One way of describing our rising sign is that it's like the clothes we wear. Our clothes convey a sense of who we are without necessarily representing our true selves. Not only does the Ascendant give an impression to others, it is also our way of dealing with life, since it shows our gut reactions to new situations and people.

Ascendants are a little more complicated than other parts of astrology because they change every couple of hours – and they are different for every Sun sign. Furthermore, they are modified by the position of the ruling planet of the Ascendant. For example: an Aries rising sign with its ruling planet, Mars, in Gemini will react to things differently than a person with an Aries rising sign where Mars is in Scorpio.

To work out our Ascendant, it is best to look online. Basically, the clock is divided into twelve two-hour segments starting at 4 in the morning. So, an Aries born at 5.07 will have a rising sign in Aries, but an Aries born at 23.36 will have a rising sign in Capricorn. For each of the twelve Sun Signs, there are twelve possible Ascendants.

DESCENDANTS

Once we have worked out our Ascendant, we automatically know our Descendant. The Descendant is what it says on the tin – the exact opposite of the Ascendant. So, a Cancer ascendant – or rising – would have Capricorn as its Descendant.

Less powerful than the Ascendant, it is a complementary opposing force. It represents a set of traits that we wouldn't normally associate with ourselves. It is that part of us that connects with other people on a one-to-one basis in our personal and professional lives. For example: it determines our attitude to marriage and partnerships, and indicates the sort of people we will get on with.

ASCENDANTS RISING

ARIES (Descendant: Libra)

Aries Ascendants are doers who act first and think later. Quick and direct, they see what they want and expect to get it. While some are competitive, mostly the competition is with themselves because they want to come first. So, they do everything quickly, and they have little patience. They are all about action. Regardless of their Sun sign, Mars is their ruler. Its location by sign and by house will describe their energy levels.

TAURUS (Descendant: Scorpio)

Hating change, Taurus Ascendants are dependable, reliable, and generous people. They are pragmatic and patient and easy-going. Plus, they love all the good things in life, so a bit of luxury is always on hand. They love to own things and view their partners as their personal property, but their calm demeanor means it's not a question of jealousy. Regardless of their Sun sign, Venus is their ruler. Its location by sign and by house describes the function of love, art, and beauty in their lives.

GEMINI (Descendant: Sagittarius)

For Gemini Ascendants, the world is about learning. They pick up information at lightning speed and are curious about everything. Often talented writers, their mind races with new ideas and thoughts, and they are easily bored. Adaptable, they love to mingle and seek out others who they find interesting. They are excitable and funny, but others can find them intimidating even though they don't mean to be. Regardless of their Sun sign, Mercury is their ruler. Its location by sign and by house describes the way they speak, learn, and the way their mind works.

CANCER (Descendant: Capricorn)

Nurturers on an epic scale, Cancer Ascendant is highly emotional and attuned to others' feelings at all times. This means they are so sensitive that it takes little to fluster them and send them retreating into their shells. Home is where their heart is and with Capricorn as their Descendant, they are looking for security and structure from their partner and in their home life. They will sacrifice anything to get it. Regardless of their Sun sign, the Moon is their ruler. Its location by sign and by house describes their emotions and instincts.

LEO (Descendant: Aquarius)

They love the limelight. Leo Ascendants are very proud people who want to be the life and soul of the party. They are born leaders who want to make things better for other people. They try not to appear too serious and are actually less confident than they appear. Their warm personality and enthusiasm acts as magnet. Regardless of their Sun sign, the Sun is their ruler. Its location by sign and by house represents their vitality and true self, which is augmented by having a Leo Ascendant.

VIRGO (Descendant: Pisces)

With an attention to detail few can rival, Virgo Ascendant is methodical and able to juggle all kinds of details and to articulate their knowledge effortlessly. They are attracted to all things intellectual, but keep their emotions to themselves. Shy, they like to analyze situations and people before they engage. They also worry endlessly about their health and are hyper-aware of any discomfort and assume the worst. Regardless of their Sun sign, Mercury is their ruler. Its location by sign and by house describes how they think and communicate.

LIBRA (Descendant: Aries)

Charming and attractive, Libra Ascendants are great company. They appear easy-going, but looks can be deceptive. Keen to keep harmony at all costs, they hate any kind of hostile environment. This means they might go through a slew of relationships before they find 'the one.' That matters because Libra Ascendants hate to be alone and much prefer being part of a couple. Regardless of their Sun sign, Venus is their ruler. Its location by sign and by house shows how central love and attraction are to them.

SCORPIO (Descendant: Taurus)

Scorpio rising is magnetism personified. People are drawn to them and they command respect although they are deeply private people. Scorpio rising are a bit like Brussel sprouts; people either love them or hate them. They divide opinion. In order to protect their privacy, they read situations and people like nobody else, so they can control their environment to the best of their ability. They are survivors. Regardless of their Sun sign, Pluto is their ruler. Its location by sign and by house rules destruction, and transformation, which is like their life.

SAGITTARIUS (Descendant: Gemini)

Always on the lookout for adventure, Sagittarius Ascendants are outgoing and restless. They take risks and embark on ambitious projects, many of which they abandon. They like to embrace different cultures and ideas. Freedom matters, and they hate to be tied down. Highly independent, they have a happy-go-lucky outlook, and little bothers them. Much of their life seems to be spent looking for something they never find. Regardless of their Sun sign, Jupiter is their ruler. Its location by sign and by house indicates areas of good fortune and opportunity.

CAPRICORN (Descendant: Cancer)

Capricorn rising hates chaos above everything. They want order and a method for everything. They are serious, reserved, and ambitious, and will work hard to achieve their goals. They have an authoritative manner and a strong moral code. Learning to relax is a challenge as they tend to be rigid and inflexible in their outlook. Ascendant personalities can be the result of family conditioning, and this is true for Capricorn rising who are often seen as the responsible ones within the family. Regardless of their Sun sign, Saturn is their ruler. Its location by sign and by house points to where they face their fears and where they create structure, so they can achieve their potential.

AQUARIUS (Descendant: Leo)

With multiple interests and multiple friends, Aquarius Ascendants are known for their cool, friendly ways. This is a bit misleading; they like to keep their distance and they hate to be pinned down. They don't care what others think about them; they tend to be a bit wary until they know people well. Naturally anti-authoritarian, they resist change and anyone who wields power. Regardless of their Sun sign, Uranus is their ruler. Its location by sign and by house highlights their rebellious nature.

PISCES (Descendant: Virgo)

Pisces rising is a dreamy, other worldly creature who can be a tad too gullible and impressionable for their own good. They have psychic abilities and artistic tendencies, and are able to turn their dreams into reality when they work hard. A tendency to wishful thinking means they can be taken for a ride a bit too easily. Regardless of their Sun sign, Neptune is their ruler. Its location by sign and by house indicates the areas of concern: spiritual fulfillment, creativity, and ideals.

CUSPS

We all have some inner conflict, but for anyone who is born on the cusp of two Zodiac signs, that's part of the territory. A cusp sign is defined as a birthday that falls on the time when the Sun leaves one sign and enters another. So, we might be an adventurous Sagittarius, but feel more like a cautious Capricorn.

Zodiac cusps are the period of several days where one sign rises as the other sets. It's actually an auspicious time to be born because it signifies moments of change and possibility, which is always a good thing.

CUSP DATES

ARIES – TAURUS	4/16 – 4/22
TAURUS – GEMINI	5/17 – 5/23
GEMINI – CANCER	6/17 – 6/23
CANCER – LEO	7/19 – 7/25
LEO – VIRGO	8/19 – 8/25
VIRGO – LIBRA	9/19 – 9/25
LIBRA – SCORPIO	10/19 – 10/25
SCORPIO – SAGITTARIUS	11/18 – 11/24
SAGITTARIUS – CAPRICORN	12/18 – 12/24
CAPRICORN – AQUARIUS	1/16 – 1/22
AQUARIUS – PISCES	2/15 – 2/21
PISCES – ARIES	3/17 – 3/23

FREE WILL

Having come this far with our understanding of how astrology works and how nuanced it is once we factor in details such as the Planets, Houses, and Ascendants, it might appear to the casual onlooker that what we are saying is that astrology has everything mapped out for us and everything is predetermined.

However, what astrology is actually telling us is that both fate (it's written in our birth charts) and free will can co-exist and do co-exist. We all know phrases such as 'what goes around, comes around,' and people who say they believe in fate and just let life happen around them. No matter how hard they try, it does seem as though they are following a predestined path. Then, there are other people who micro-manage and control every aspect of their life, and life just seems to do as they want. There is also a third group of people, which, let's be honest, will be most of us, where it seems as though free will and fate co-exist. How many times have we heard the phrase, 'it was fate' or 'it was meant to happen,' when someone does something out of the ordinary and it has consequences? Say, they meet the love of their lives at a party they weren't meant to attend but then did at the last moment. Is that their free will operating, or is it fate intervening? And how does astrology deal with both concepts?

One branch of astrology believes that the amount of fate or free will in a person's life can be seen in their birth charts and depends on the position of the planets in our charts. If we divide the chart into eastern and western houses (west on the left, east on the right), then any planets located on the left side of the line (where our Ascendant is) is our free will, and anything on the right of the line (where our Descendant is) is our fate.

The so-called Eastern Hemisphere represents our self-determination and will power and our ability to determine outcomes. The Western Hemisphere represents the twists of fate, immovable powers, and the established forces in our lives. How many planets sit in each half will

determine how much free will we have; the more that lie in the east, the more the power of our will is. Likewise, the more in the west, the more we are in the hands of fate.

Knowing this is important because it allows us to take control of our lives. If we are predominantly western-based, then we can learn that being flexible and going with the flow is ultimately the best way forward. So, if work asks us to relocate, rather than waste energy fighting it, we see it as a new opportunity and embrace it.

Ultimately, life is what we make of it. Sit home all day, watching television – and not much will happen. Get out there and make the most of everything – good and bad – and life is suddenly in our own hands. Astrology just shows us that it's all happening for a reason. It tells us we have choices, and with a new perspective, anything is possible. It is there to protect us and guide us.

FINDING INSIGHT

Many of us read our daily horoscope. Reading this each day is fun, but a daily horoscope does little more than scratch the surface of astrology's potential. To really understand how astrology works, a birth chart is essential.

A birth chart is unique. It is a once-only, never-to-be-repeated arrangement of planets, signs, and houses, as well as more specialized astrological details such as angles and aspects. Reading a horoscope is easy, reading an astrological chart is less so. Fortunately, our guide will make it as easy as possible to understand.

Firstly, a birth chart is a guide; it contains all the information we need to help us fulfill our potential. It helps us to understand ourselves better, so we can fully express our true selves. What makes the birth chart unique is that it is exactly what it says it is: a chart taken at the precise moment and location of birth.

The planets are constantly moving, and, at the time of birth, they will all occupy a particular place. It will be the same for anyone born at that time anywhere on Earth. However, once we factor in the location of birth (expressed in longitude and latitude), the charts of two people born at the same time will have different angles and house cusps. They are a different version of the same arrangement of planets in the sky. Even when twins are born, perhaps only a few minutes apart, the difference in time means that a planet might have moved into a different house, or the angles might have moved into the next Zodiac sign.

There is something mysterious and other-worldly about a birth chart. At first glance, it looks a bit like a segmented pie, with some of the segments empty and others full of strange-looking glyphs and numbers. Add on the angles and letters and it can all add up to look like gobbledygook. In ancient times, astrologers cast birth charts by hand using an ephemeris and a table of houses.

Today, it is so much easier thanks to the internet and astrological software!

PREPARING YOUR BIRTH CHART

To create a birth chart, we need the following: exact birth date (day, month and year) and time and place of birth. It's best to use a birth certificate, where possible, rather than rely on memory. The time of birth affects everything, so it's important to be as accurate as possible. Place of birth means the town or village, not the precise street. That's because we need to know the longitude and latitude.

Once we have the information, it's incredibly easy to plot our precise birth charts now with internet access.

INTERPRETING A BIRTH CHART

When we look at our chart we can see where our rising (Ascendant) sign is located. We can also see which signs and planets are in which houses. There is also much more detail such as where our modes and nodes are located and which, if any, planets are in retrograde.

It's more than likely we already know our Sun sign, but if we don't, it's clear to see in the chart. We also need to find our Moon sign because that is the first step to interpreting our chart. Remember, our Sun and Moon signs are our central drives. We need to look at them by sign, house, and aspect, and also note which house each of them rules.

On a birth chart, each planet and each Zodiac sign is represented by its glyph. It's important to learn these because it makes it much easier than looking them up every time. If that is too much, copy them onto a crib sheet so they are easy to refer to each time a new glyph appears.

THE ASCENDANT SIGN

This will be marked by AC. Remember, it is significant because it is the sign that was rising on the eastern horizon at our birth (and it is always located at 9 o'clock). It takes the Ascendant and Descendant two hours, on average, to move through each sign, which is why the more accurate the birth time given, the more accurate the chart. The Ascendant dictates how we view the world and how the world views us, and it always appears in the first house. We can then calculate the position of all our houses because they always run counter-clockwise.

Opposite the Ascendant sign is our Descendant sign. Note which sign and house it sits in. The line linking the two is the horizon line. If a large number of planets are above the horizon line, we are more likely to be an extrovert who looks to the world for confirmation and recognition. If the majority of the planets are below the line, we are introverted and shy away from public life in favor of our privacy.

We can further divide our chart by placing the MC or Midheaven at 12 o'clock and the IC or Imum Coeli at 6 o'clock. The MC and IC move through each Zodiac sign in exactly two hours. If more planets sit to the left (the eastern side), we are independent and a self-starter, while to the right (the western side), we are more dependent on circumstances. Most people do, in fact, have a mixture of planets on each side.

THE RULING PLANET

Once we have looked at our Sun and Moon locations, we can study the remaining personal planets. They are Mercury, Venus, and Mars (which complete the rest of the details about our personality), as well as Jupiter and Saturn, called the social planets, which describe our experiences out in the world. One of these planets will be our ruling planet; whichever rules our Ascendant is the ruler of our chart. This determines how people see us and also what we think about ourselves. It is key to our understanding because it trumps everything else that is happening in our chart.

ASCENDANT SIGN	RULING PLANET	HOW WE PRESENT OURSELVES
Aries	Mars	Strong-willed, impetuous
Taurus	Venus	Stable, sensuous
Gemini	Mercury	Articulate, highly-strung
Cancer	Moon	Emotional, empathetic
Leo	Sun	Confident, full of life
Virgo	Mercury	Organized, discriminating
Libra	Venus	Equitable, charming
Scorpio	Pluto/Mars	Controlled, reserved
Sagittarius	Jupiter	Adventurous, excitable
Capricorn	Saturn	Proud, respectable
Aquarius	Uranus/Saturn	Off-beat, friendly
Pisces	Neptune/Jupiter	Idealistic, sensitive

If we then look at which house our ruling planet sits in, we can refine our knowledge further. So, let's quickly summarize what each house says and then use that to show how the house position influences us.

RULING PLANET IN	PERSONALITY
First House	Self-starter, stand-out personality
Second House	High morals, money-maker
Third House	Good communicator, gossip
Fourth House	Homebody, family person
Fifth House	Devoted parent, romantic, entertainer
Sixth House	Perfectionist, workaholic, worrier
Seventh House	Companion, confidante
Eighth House	Questioner, observer
Ninth House	Thinker, explorer
Tenth House	Achiever, in the public eye
Eleventh House	Friend, community minded
Twelfth House	Recluse, spiritually-focused

DISCOVERING DESTINY

But how can we apply what we have learned from our birth chart to our ability to read the future? The ancients used their charts and their knowledge. For millennia, rulers and leaders would not act until they had consulted their astrologers for advice and had their horoscopes read. This was based on the concept, as we have seen, that no chart is ever still. The planets continue to orbit around, producing transits over our particular planets, houses, and angles, meaning that energy changes from moment to moment. Our aim in this book is not to read the future of a nation, however, just ourselves! Let's work out how we can create our own horoscope to forecast our own future.

TRANSITS

The key tools to forecasting in astrology are transits. They reflect the present, but they also reflect the past and what the future may hold. A transit is a crossing, when a planet moves across something on our chart. After the moment of birth, the planets move on; they enter and leave houses, they cross angles and they form aspects to other planets, resulting in a continual dynamism.

At any moment, transits will highlight certain areas in our charts. They will reflect how we feel at that moment, and reveal the true meaning of the things that happen to us and how to respond to them. Every different planetary movement means something slightly different; when a planet transits in conjunction it can enter a number of (technical) aspects, each with its own particular resonance.

CHECKING OUR TRANSITS

For this, we need to consult the internet once again. Certain websites contain all the planetary positions for around ten thousand years, so locating the information should not be a problem.

Remember that, with the exception of the Sun and the Moon, all the planets go retrograde at some point in their cycle. This means that they can pass over a point on a birth chart several times. Pluto, Neptune, and Uranus transits take more than a year and they bring with them the biggest changes. Jupiter, Saturn, and the comet Chiron's transits are also significant, but they are shorter while Mars, Venus, and Mercury happen very frequently with numerous retrogrades.

CREATING A HOROSCOPE

Taking what we know about the details of astrology and each Sun sign, the best way to write a horoscope is by looking at planetary activity and then working out how this activity affects each sign in turn. For example: a disruptive Mercury transit combined with a full Moon will affect sensitive Pisces more than bullish Sagittarius. What we want to know from the planets is how they affect us on every level of our lives, from our relationships, to our home life and work.

The second thing to remember is that horoscopes are different depending on the timeframe. A daily horoscope is different from a weekly or a monthly one. Depending on what kind of horoscope we want, we need to look at transits happening on a certain day, or across a week, a month, or a year. The key is to look for connections between the movements of the planets and each sign's nature. What a good general chart should do is to find the most significant point attached to a sign and then explore it. For instance, if Mercury is retrograde, that will not bother an easy-going Gemini as much as a set-in-their-ways Taurus.

IT'S NOT ABOUT PREDICTING THE FUTURE

We all turn to our horoscopes to see what our immediate or near future holds. In fact, if we read a horoscope correctly, we will see that the horoscope's predictions aren't really telling us our future. What they are doing is showing what might be happening now, or soon, so that we can better understand our moods and be more equipped to deal with these situations. So, the prediction of an argument at work with your boss doesn't mean you are going to be sacked; it is a prediction that allows us to foresee a potentially difficult situation, in order to avoid it becoming a worse situation. Horoscopes, as with astrology, are tools for self-awareness.

WE ALL HAVE A CHOICE

As we have seen throughout this long journey into learning about astrology, it is all about choices, which are as unique as each one of us. Use astrology wisely and it will show us how we can alter our reality by changing our perspective and using our understanding to reimagine our approach to life. Astrology guides us. It gives us signposts so that we can weigh up the information and then act accordingly. It helps us to understand why some days things don't go as we had hoped and other days everything falls into place.

Astrology is our pathway into creating our own destiny.

ASTROLOGY GLOSSARY

air sign: Gemini, Libra, Aquarius; intellectual, always on the go, the realm of communication.

angles: These are the Ascendant (ASC), Descendant (DSC), Midheaven (MC), and Imum Coeli (IC). Each refers to the cusps of the first, seventh, tenth, and fourth houses, respectively.

Ascendant: Also known as the rising sign, this is the sign on the cusp of the First House of the birth chart. It is the sign and degree of the sign, which is rising on the eastern horizon at the exact moment of birth.

aspect: The angle planets make with each other, creating a certain type of relationship or connection as they move in their elongated orbits around the Sun.

birth chart: A diagram that represents the position of planets at the moment a person was born. The planet's positioning holds important information about a person's life. It is also known as a 'natal chart.'

cusp: The boundary between two houses in the chart. It is also when one sign ends and the other begins.

cycle: A full circuit of a planet around a chart or in relation to another planet.

Descendant: The cusp of the seventh house of the astrology chart: it sits directly opposite the Ascendant.

earth sign: Taurus, Virgo, Capricorn; grounded, practical, the realm of material things.

eclipse: An eclipse happens when the Earth, Moon, and Sun line up in the sky. They happen a few times a year and are linked to dramatic and unexpected changes in our lives.

elements: The twelve Zodiac signs are grouped into four elements: air, earth, fire, and water. Each Zodiac sign is connected to one of the elements.

ephemeris: A listing of planetary positions each day at midday or at midnight. It also records information about lunar phases and eclipses.

fire sign: Aries, Leo, Sagittarius; passionate, confident, the realm of creation.

glyphs: these are the symbols used for the astrological signs, planets, luminaries, and aspects.

horoscope: Forecast of a person's future based on the position of the planets and stars at the time of birth.

house: Along with the twelve signs, the Zodiac wheel is also divided up into twelve houses, pie-chart style. Each house has rulership over specific areas of life.

Imum Coeli: Or IC, is the point in space where the ecliptic crosses the Meridian in the north. It is located exactly opposite the Midheaven.

luminaries: The Sun and the Moon.

Midheaven: Or MC, this is the sign on the cusp of the tenth house of the birth chart. It is the highest point in the Zodiac at the moment of birth.

modalities: These are the different forms of expression of the Zodiac signs: Cardinal (enterprising and initiate change: Aries, Cancer, Libra, and Capricorn), Fixed (focused and determined: Taurus, Leo, Scorpio, and Aquarius) and Mutable (flexible and versatile: Gemini, Virgo, Sagittarius, and Pisces).

natal chart: See birth chart.

nodes: The point in the Zodiac where a planet, particularly the Moon, passes from southern into northern latitudes is called the North Node, and when moving in the opposite direction (crossing from north to south) is called the South Node.

orb: The space in Zodiac degrees either side of an exact aspect between two planets.

planetary rulers: Each sign is ruled by a planet.

quadrants: A chart has four quadrants, and each starts at the cusp of the first, fourth, seventh, and tenth houses.

retrograde: A planet is considered "retrograde" when it appears to be moving backwards. This is an optical illusion and occurs when the Earth overtakes a slower-moving planet or is overtaken by a faster-moving planet. It is often associated with things going haywire. Retrograde periods are opportunities to slow down and consider things.

stellium: A cluster of stars within the same sign or house or within a certain orb in adjacent houses. Any sign or house with three or more planets is significant.

table of houses: A reference book used by astrologers when calculating birth charts by hand and not using astrology software.

transit: The movement of a planet around the chart. There are usually at least a few transits happening on any given day. Each planet moves through houses and crosses over planets, angles, and other chart points.

water sign: Cancer, Scorpio, Pisces; compassionate, sensitive, the realm of emotion.

Zodiac: The circle of animals based on the twelve main constellations, which lie along the Sun's path during a calendar year.